APOCALYPSE THEN

(Not Now)

Indexing the Apocalypse

By

L. Michael Hall, Ph.D.

E.T. Publications
1904 N. 7th. Street
Grand Junction   Colorado   81501-7418   USA

© *1994 L. Michael Hall, Ph.D.*
Original Title: The Cure For Millennial Madness

Register of Copyrights TX 3 851-841

Third Edition (February, 1997)

Table of Contents

Introduction to Third Edition	4
Introduction to Second Edition	6
Introduction	8
1. **Indexing** *Checking Out When, Where, What, Who, Why*	10
2. **Indexing WHEN** *The Time Element*	24
3. **Indexing WHERE** *The Socio-Political Environment*	39
4. **Indexing WHAT** *The Jewish Holocaust of AD 70*	51
5. **Indexing WHO** *Romans Chapters 9-11*	72
6. **Indexing WHO** *The Epistle of Hebrews*	83
7. **Indexing the Literary Style** *Apocalyptism As A Literary Device*	112
8. **Indexing The Significance** *"So What?"*	130
9. **Indexing the How** *The Process of the End (Revelation)*	160
10. **Indexing the Consequences of This Paradigm** *What does this Mean for Us Today?*	172
Finale: Indexing the Psychological "Madness"	187
Appendix A: *Reality and Shadows*	192
Other Available Resources	196
Bibliography	198

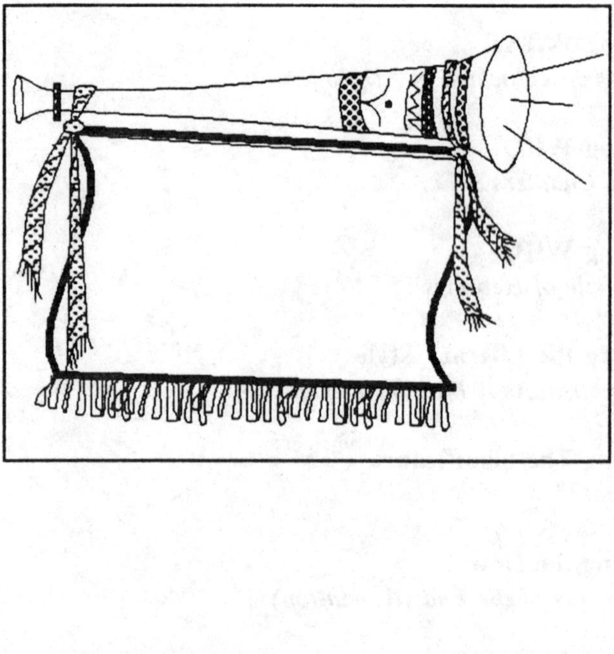

Introduction to Third Edition

This work began in 1985 with a little pamphlet that I entitled *"AD 70."* At that time I did not take the "full" preterist viewpoint. By the writing of *"The Cure For Millennial Madness"* (1993) I had adopted the fulfilled eschatology viewpoint.

As both supporters and detractors responded to the book, I found myself studying and restudying the matter. The dispensationalists who disliked the findings and wanted to argue against it all spoke against it as violating their *literal sense of biblical fulfillment.* This seemed the foundation of all their hermeneutics--they read and perceived scriptures through a literalistic filter. Nearly all of them would write to say, "I take the Bible to mean what it says and say what it means."

Of course, that ploy would completely do away with the entire realm of *interpretation (hermeneutics).* Yet that precisely describes the phenomenon that we cannot do away with. Why not? Because **meaning** does not exist in words but arises as a function of a human mind as it gives some significance (meaning) to something and then communicates that via words, linguistic structures, contexts, contexts-of-contexts, etc.

Accordingly, to get the author's original meaning, we as listeners and recipients of his or her words and literature have to engage in a literary process--that of discerning that meaning. The danger in this arises because we (as meaning makers as well) tend to bring our filters, meanings, beliefs, values, presuppositions, etc. to the text. We cannot do otherwise. To manage this process, we need to become *conscious of our perceptual filters* so that we can not become blinded by them.

This work invites you essentially to become aware of your own interpretative filters and offers you a hermeneutical tool (*indexing*) that can enable you to deal more honestly with the historical-grammatical nature of the biblical text. As you do that I think it will lead you to a new viewpoint about biblical eschatology.

Now for a story. **Alan Deutsch** became one of the first persons to respond to the first edition of the book. He thought it "most useful, succinct and powerful." He further said that he would love to see the book "dressed in some outlandishly slick cover and widely distributed...with a new title like 'The Late Great planet Israel'..."

Later while working on my doctorate, Alan kept nudging me to put out a new edition and to dress it up. So I began rewriting the entire work, expanding it, and writing it in E-prime (English primed of the "to be" verbs, a literary device from general-semantics). Then it sat – until Alan took "the bull by the horns" (so to speak) and made this edition possible. So I dedicate this book to –

Alan Deutsch
*For his excitement and courage and faith
in making* **Apocalypse Then** *possible*

David Rossiter
For nudging me in this direction in the first place

Roger D. Rossiter
For his challenges and friendship

Charles Geiser
For his initial challenges

and

Max King & Ed Stevens
*For their personal encouragement
and their insightful writings in preterism*

Introduction to the Second Edition

With this edition, I have expanded and extended the chapter that addresses indexing the consequences of this eschatological paradigm. When people ask, *"What difference does it make anyway?"* I enjoy answering, "In the ultimate scheme of things --none. It really doesn't. God will ultimately do whatever he will do and neither my thoughts, theology, theologizing, etc. nor yours will effect that."

I equally enjoy then adding, "On the immediate and personal level, one's view about biblical eschatology *makes a lot of difference*. It radically affects one's thoughts, feelings, and experiences regarding the new covenant, grace, law, the gospel's empowerment, the nature of Christianity, etc."

One of the most convincing pieces for me involves the question regarding the existence, or non-existence, of *the new covenant age*, whether it now exists or whether we wait for it as a future hope. Has God fulfilled the promises of Jeremiah 31:31-34 or not? Does Hebrews 8:6-13 and II Corinthians 3-5 speak about current reality or future reality? If they speak about the current Christian age, then how do their fulfillment differ from the fulfillment of the new covenant descriptions in Revelation 21- 22:5? A contrastive analysis between these texts inevitably puts a great burden on the person who claims that Revelation 21-22 as yet future.

After writing the first edition, Ed Stevens teased my mind with "the water of life" passage in Ezekiel 47. If that stream that flows from the temple in the messianic age refers to "the river of the water of life" that flows from the throne of God and of the Lamb (Rev. 22:1ff) for the healing of the nations, then perhaps *the deepening of the waters* in Ezekiel's vision after measurements of a thousand (47:3-12) may refer to the deepening and broadening of the knowledge of God about the everlasting covenant in Christ.

Accordingly, in the first thousand years, this knowledge would only become ankle-deep. By the second millennium it would become knee-deep. By the third, "it was up to the loins," and by the fourth, "it was a river that I could not pass through…"

Whether that reflects the passage true meaning or not, it certainly stands true that *the realized eschatology view that uses spiritual eyes to see the kingdom of God in our midst and permeating our world* only now seems knee-deep… and yet growing. When the Twenty-ninth and Thirtieth centuries comes, I would find it interesting to know what view Christians will then take of this.

A more critical view about eschatology concerns what your view does to you mentally, emotionally, and personally. Does your view lead to a "spirit of power, love and sound mind" (II Timothy 1:7)? Does it empower your everyday life? Does it make you more Christlike and able to take effective action in the world? Or does it lead to "a spirit of fear?" If it does, it does **not** represent the biblical view.

Introduction

APOCALYPSE THEN

(i.e. Not Now)

Indexing the "End of the World"

Will the world *soon* come to an end? Or did "the end of the world" already occur? Will Jesus return to bring an end to the world in a baptism of fire? Or did he already do that in AD 70 when he consummated the kingdom? Will there yet come some horrible tribulation that will devastate the world? Or did that already happened in the AD 70 Jewish holocaust? Will there yet arise some terrible antichrist who will bring darkness upon the planet? Or did Nero and the first-century Judaizers already do that?

These eschatology questions structurally posit two sets of very different answers, do they not? The one you choose as making the most sense will make a lot of difference in your thinking, feeling, responding, and overall Christian experience.

If you posit the return of Christ for resurrection, judgment, kingdom, etc. into *some yet unknown future*--you thereby assume that all of the tribulation, persecution, dark times, terrible beasts, etc. of Revelation still looms on the horizon as something yet to come. **Horrors!** And you call that "good news?" With this view you look upon the New Testament and the book of *Revelation* as loaded with some very sober, grim, and negative predictions. No wonder this view tends to generate **millennial madness**! No wonder it encourages a Christian perspective strongly tainted by paranoia and pessimism toward the world, a negative and withdrawing response to the current socio-political situation, and a fearful orientation of dread of the future.

What objections do I have to all that? Namely that it discounts the *"at hand" statements* of the early Christians which you find everywhere in the biblical text. It also stands absolutely contrary to Paul's description of the Judeo-Christian spirit. In his letter to Timothy, Paul said that "God has *not* given us the spirit of fear, but of power, love, and sound mind" (II Timothy 1:7).

Now I don't think it will come to you as a great secret that the early Hebrew believers experienced themselves and their world from *an end-time perspective*. They absolutely believed that their world would come to an end within their lifetime. Where did they get such an idea? Did it come true? Did it represent the true state of affairs?

Their end-time thinking and believing came from Jesus and his apostles who talked and wrote in such terms. Do you think they erred? Did they speak the truth? Accepting the biblical record for what it *says* forces us to address this question. Exploring the theology of covenant, Israel, and Israel's messiah mandates that we reconcile their expectations with history. Did they indeed live in the last days? The last days of what? Did their world exist on the verge of a great cataclysmic holocaust of great tribulation? Did the apostles speak truth when they asserted that such things stood *"at hand?"* How should we understand these things today? Do we conclude that them on target or sadly mistaken? If their view on this aspect of their message demonstrates error pure and simple, what shall we say about the other parts of their message? If their views represented reality, how shall we understand them as correct? In what way did a world end?

Chapter 1

**

INDEXING

THE APOCALYPSE

Checking Out The When, Where, Who, What, How, & Why of "the End of the World"

All of the questions in the previous paragraph do not only apply to the apostles and followers. **Jesus himself** staked *the veracity of his gospel* on this message about the end-times in his generation. Unequivocally he asserted such.

> "Truly I say to you, this generation will not pass away till all these things take place" (Matt. 24:34-5). "When you see these things taking place, you know that the kingdom of God is near" (Luke 21:31). "Truly, I say to you, there are some standing here who will not taste death before they see the Son of man coming in his kingdom" (Matt. 16:27-28).

The apostles also, in line with this apocalyptic vision, amplified what Jesus said. John left no doubt about it.

> "*It is the last time*: and as you have heard that antichrist shall come, *even now* there are many antichrists; whereby we know that it is the last time" (I John 2:18).

For him, he would not have to wait thousands of years for the antichrists; antichrists represented a present reality.

He also asserted that the end as imminent in his time. "The revelation of Jesus Christ to show what **must soon take place**... **the time is near**" (Rev. 1:1-3, see 22:6,7,10, 12, 20). Nor did doubt cross Peter's mind that the events would shortly wrap up everything.

10

"The end of all things is at hand..." (I Pet. 4:7). "Set your hope fully upon the grace that is coming to you at the revelation of Jesus Christ" (1:13, II Peter 3:10-14). James, Jesus' brother in the flesh, asserted the same, "Establish your hearts, for the coming of the Lord is at hand" (James 5:8).

Nor did scholarly Paul temper these wild-eye predictions from those less educated about an imminent end of that age. Everywhere in his theology, he spoke of the end as "at hand."

"The mystery of iniquity is *already at work*" (II Thess. 2:7, I Thess. 1:9-10, 5:1-4). "Knowing the time, that now it is high time to awake out of sleep; for now is our salvation nearer than when we believed..." (Rom. 13:11-12). "The God of peace shall bruise Satan under your feet shortly" (Rom. 16:20). "The appointed time has grown very short... The form of this world is passing away." (I Cor. 7:29,31). These things "were written down for our instruction, upon whom *the end of the ages has come*" (I Cor. 10:11).

In Hebrews, the writer not only identified the last days, ("In these last days he has spoken to us by a Son..." 1:2), but he also specified, "What is becoming obsolete and growing old [the old covenant] *is ready to vanish away*" (8:13). Accordingly, he thought it urgent that they "not neglecting to meet together...and all the more as you see the Day drawing near") (10:25).

"For yet a little while, and the coming one shall come and shall not tarry..." (10:37, also 12:18-29).

These quotes make all of those originators sound like a bunch of fanatics, do they not? After reading these scriptures and many like them, do you have any question in your mind that *they all shared an imminent vision of the end*? How shall we explain this? What did they believe? Did Jesus return and bring an end to the world or not? Did his words come true that all those things happened before that generation passed and while some standing there still lived or not?

WELCOME TO THE WILD AND WONDERFUL WORLD OF ESCHATOLOGY

These *time-statements* about "the end" have to, literally, do with the theological field called *eschatology*. This domain refers to "the study of last things" ("eschatos" comes from Greek and means "last").

But what last things? The last things of this or that civilization? The last things of this or that covenant? The last things of the planet and human civilization? Obviously, when we do not *index the subject and content* regarding the referent under discussion, we make it possible for people to hallucinate all kinds of things into that fuzzy void. In the field of biblical interpretation, that explains precisely what has happened that has created the present day confusion about eschatology. People have failed to index, or contextualize, the scripture as they read.

Generation after generation have, for hundreds even thousands of years, *failed to index* those "end of the world" time-statements. What consequence has come of this? Every generation has thought of itself as the last generation! So people keep saying, "Yep, the coming of Christ must really be soon now!" Entire movements and denominations have arisen around a commitment to a specific end-time date. And yet, *every prophecy* of the end of the world in modern times has proven false! Not most of them--**every single one of them!** Now I would call that "a terrible track record!" 100% of the prophecies have failed.

The time has come for us to *call into question* the underlying presuppositions behind today's "end of the world" prophecies. Let's challenge the very assumptions upon which people have based all of the current fears and paranoia about "the end." Let's take a closer look at the biblical texts from which we have mined our ideas to check them for the time-frame of the original authors.

The traditional viewpoint about eschatology starts from *the assumption* that the biblical statements about the end refer to some yet future event. How valid should we estimate that assumption? Upon what basis do we jump to such conclusions? What if the "end of the world" statements *in context* do not refer to some event beyond the time-frame of the first century?

What if we found that by *indexing the statements to the time and place* where the authors wrote them, and in reference to an event (or set of events) imminent at that time we find that their world did come to an end at the termination of a great tribulation and that all of the signs predicting that end took place precisely as Jesus and his apostles prophesied? What if we found such?

Wouldn't that change everything? Yes! Then, instead of "the end of the world" and the coming of the kingdom not yet having come, we would discover with eyes wide open to **how** the kingdom *has come* in its fullness. That would enable us to allow that kingdom, and all of the redemption events that it brought to come more completely into our lives. Then, we could appreciate more fully for how God has wrapped things up, brought in his new covenant, and initiated the completeness of the Christian reality.

AN ESCHATOLOGICAL PARADIGM SHIFT

The phrase *"paradigm shift"* appears currently in business, management, leadership, psychology, and theology literature. It refers to *one's model* or mental map of something. It refers to one's "way of thinking," perceptual frame-of-reference, world-view, etc.

If we begin thinking that "the end of the world" that the biblical writers described as "at hand" as having come upon them in the first century--*that would create a tremendous paradigm shift*. To adopt this paradigm shift, you must shift from thinking that *the spiritual reality of the new covenant* has not come, to believing that it has.

How easy would a radical shift of perspective like that settle in your thinking? It would totally challenge the old "the kingdom is not here" paradigm. It would mean we do not have to wait around any longer for "the second coming;" it exists as a present reality. It would mean we could do away with all the negative apocalyptic thinking about the world with its Greek anti-materialism orientation, its "on-hold" style of waiting around until the "reality" comes, and a "being so heavenly minded that one becomes of no earthly good."

I used to believe such things. I received my initial theological training in that school of thought. Over the years, however, questions from the biblical text kept challenging me to re-examine such assumptions. Eventually my research took me to a radically new perspective that completely reframed my understandings of the new covenant. In the end, it set me free from the negativism and passivism of the "end-of-the-world" fanaticism so characteristic of many believers.

You may, or may not, agree with my conclusions here. Getting you to does not represent my primary objective. Of course, I'd like for you to agree with this viewpoint, yet even more important, I simply desire that you *give thoughtful, intelligent, and insightful consideration* to this alternative view. I seek primarily to challenge and sharpen your interpretative skills so that you can think and converse with clarity of mind about the biblical text.

In facilitating this, I will offer some perspectives on hermeneutics, biblical history, the socio-political context of the New Testament scriptures, some Hebraic viewpoints about the biblical text, an integration of gospel and theology, some factual details on the AD 70 holocaust, etc. Ultimately, you will have to come to your own conclusions. Such represents not only your right but also your responsibility in "being fully persuaded in your own mind" (Romans 14:5). I pray that may it stand as a conviction informed, intelligible, and conscientious.

After the first edition, I received numerous letters from people who strongly disagreed. Some took to name calling. I supposed that somehow they thought that would provide a rational argument for their view. Several quickly read the material and immediately shot off a hot missive to "set me straight." When I engaged such persons about what they thought my main argument within the book--they could not state it. All they knew focused on their negative judgment; they did not like it. Yet they had not read closely enough to even state it in their own words with accuracy. Obviously, if a person wants to argue against other's point of view, they should become well enough informed as to have the ability to accurate represent that perspective.

HOW I SHIFTED MY THINKING PARADIGM ABOUT NEW COVENANT ESCHATOLOGY

My own shift of perspective took seven years. The shift grew slowly, piece by piece. It took time to flush out the presuppositions that gave rise to the older traditional views. Only gradually did I start challenging and deframing those presuppositions.

Scholars identify the perspective offered here as *the preterist view* of fulfilled eschatology or covenant eschatology. When I first heard it, I questioned it vigorously. In a knee-jerk reaction fashion, I reacted against it. But it raised questions that the traditional views had difficulty addressing. As I researched, I found that many facets of the preterist viewpoint I could easily affirm and so began to hold it tentatively on some points. Since that initial shifting and trying on of this eschatological paradigm, I have spent fifteen years exploring how this view fits into the whole of the biblical text. I now feel convinced of its correctness and esteem it as an insightful model.

As a disclaimer, I recognize that this model does not answer every question about every passage regarding New Testament eschatology. *No current model will do that.* So what will it do? It will offer a more consist perspective in integrating with the context of the NT regarding such important themes as the coming of the new covenant, grace, forgiveness, justification by grace through faith, the good-news, etc.

If you receive no other learning from this work than information about the Jewish Holocaust of AD 70, I encourage you to read this for the purpose of understanding the crucial events of AD 70 *in terms of biblical history*. In that year the Romans burned the Temple to the ground and, to this day, it has remained destroyed. Several have tried to rebuild it, no one has.

AD 70 marks the year when Christianity became finally and completely severed from Judaism. After that year, no one in the civilized world would confuse the two. If this sounds familiar, it should. Jesus spoke about these things in his famous Olivet Discourse. There he said "one stone would not be left upon another" when the world would end. And that became true with a vengeance at the fall of Jerusalem and the Jewish holocaust from the Jewish-Roman War of AD 66-72 (Matt. 24:1-2ff). That year brought an end to apostolic Christianity inasmuch as no apostle survived that holocaust.

AD 70 also served as the year the Romans drove the Jews out of their historical land and forbid them entrance. A thousand years later the Crusades tried to reverse the fate of that year. That represented the time when the old covenant, which had become "old" by the cross, finally became "obsolete and vanished" (Hebrews 8:13).

How much do you know about an event that had such ramifications? You will find it alluded to again and again in Bible dictionaries, commentaries, and other works when you read about Jerusalem, the temple, Judaism, the apostolic age, the Roman Empire, Nero, the persecution of the early Christians, the "soon" and "at hand" statements in the Bible, the apocalypse of Matthew 24, etc.

INDEXING THE HERMENEUTIC QUESTION

Open the Bible and what do you find? A book *not very easy to understand*! Why Not? It has all kinds of weird names, images, ideas, and referents. It suddenly throws you back into a different time and age. Suddenly you find yourself in an ancient and primitive world. In this strange world people speak a different language and express a cultural norm very different from our own. Their customs don't fit many of today's customs.

Accordingly, to understand the language, ideas, and referents of the Bible, *you have to index* its linguistics. This means that you have to probe its language, words, word-forms, sentence syntax, etc. to find out what a given author had reference to in his allusions. This means asking basic *hermeneutical questions* in order to first discover what the author meant.

In seeking to understanding and accurately interpret the literature of the New Testament Scriptures you need to index the features of the data.

- *What happened* --the content of the data
- *When spoken* --time of the writing
- *When information would occur*--time reference
- *Where*--the socio-political, religious environment
- *Who* --the recipients of the message
- *How* --the method or process of the events
- *Why* --the reasons, motivations, meanings
- *In what way* --the style of communicating the events

Only by such *indexing*, will you contextualize the written material and gain a clear understanding of what the author originally intended to communicate. To fail to do this lends not only to misunderstanding of its communication, but misusing and actual distortion. A "text out of context" almost always functions as a pretext for ideas and opinions imposed upon it.

This explains why (and how) you can prove almost anything with the Bible. *If* you deal with a text that you do not index and contextualize, if you do not put coordinates on the time, place, author, literature, etc., the words of the text can easily become distorted and made to sound like whatever message you desire. Hence, "I will accept no bull from your house..." (Psalm 50:9). Don't you think that carried a different message in context than what it sounds like today?

This indexing process not only holds true for the Bible; it holds true for all literature. *Quote someone out of context* and you have the potentiality for gross distortion of the message. When did that person say it? A quote from his eight year old self will differ greatly from 30 or 50 year old self. From what context did that statement arise? To whom? Etc.

Now when you consider that the biblical authors wrote their texts in languages long dead, in a culture and world that no longer exists, by people and to people that we sometimes have little information about, that dealt with referents now buried in ancient history, do not these principles of indexing (contextualizing) become even more important if we want to gain accurate understanding?

When you open the Bible, the writers usher you into a world very different from your everyday world. Opening the biblical text immerses you into a story that occurred in a far away time and place, characterized by strange customs, language, thought patterns, history, referents, etc. To open its pages sets you down in a different world, time, and culture. It time-travels you far before the modern industrial age to a time when the world existed in a much more barbaric state.

Opening the pages of the NT suddenly time-travels you to the days of the Roman Empire and into one of its small provinces. Here you experience a nation which intensely hated the experience of living under Roman dominance and occupation and which impatiently awaited their Messiah to deliver them from the present world and usher in the long-awaited "kingdom of God" that would fulfill the covenant promises to Abraham.

All this challenges the person wanting to interpret and understand the Bible. The Bible, as you undoubtedly already know, does not actually represent one book, but a multiple book comprised of many books (66) and therefore many *literary genre* (different kinds of literature). Nor did these writings arise at the same time. They authors wrote them at different times and places in response to particular needs. Accordingly, to understand any given piece of biblical literature --you need to know *who* wrote it, *when* that author wrote it, *to whom*, *about what*, *for what* purpose or objective, etc.

Unless you take the time to do *this careful kind of indexing of the referents*, the words will mislead you to erroneous conclusions. As with the language of any specialized field, if you don't know how the author uniquely and specially uses his or her words, you will inevitably misunderstand the communication. Without doing the literary work of exploring the meaning of the words, your thinking and perceiving will demonstrate sloppiness, laziness, and inaccuracy.

To do this kind of literary exploration forces you to enter the domain that is called *exegesis*. This discipline studies how to interpret and understand an author's meanings, intentions, words, style, etc. which you find in the text given his background, linguistic style, etc. If you don't do exegesis, you will end up doing what many do--*eisegesis*. This means *reading your own preconceived ideas into* a text! ("Ex" means "out," whereas "eis" means "in" or "into.") This does not represent wisdom if your objective involves discovering what the Bible says and what it means in its sayings.

This explains the importance of the domain of study called *hermeneutics*. This "science of biblical interpretation" arises from the need to understand the literature as a communication piece utilizing various literary devices for conveying and packaging meaning. (see *"Hermeneutics: Literary Devices that Open Up the Scriptures"*).

Hermeneutics, as a study and disciplines, stands as a necessity for understanding any literature. When you read any piece of literature, from the newspaper to the Sunday comics, to a textbook on auto repair, you engage in a hermeneutical task. This means you begin with numerous *assumptions* about how the literature works, how to read it, how to discern its meaning, etc. These assumptions comprise the principles you begin with that function as *the intellectual keys* that open a text to your understanding. Yet they arise from one's presuppositions about language (linguistics), meaning (semantics), and communication (information processing, coding, and outputting).

HERMENEUTICAL PRESUPPOSITIONS

If reading literature in general demands the reader engage in a hermeneutical task because to read presupposes we inescapably make numerous assumptions about words, language, context, etc. then the wisest thing we can do involves making this process conscious. By making it conscious, we can then evaluate it. For whether our presuppositions operate consciously or unconsciously, they nevertheless inevitably serve as our *operational hermeneutics*. By them we "make sense" of the words we read. If your operational hermeneutics function as the determining elements guiding and explaining how we will interpret a text, then understanding and elevating our linguistic presuppositions becomes inherently important.

As a science and art, our hermeneutics enables us to properly handle metaphor phrases (i.e. "he was tickled pink") without literalizing. It enables us to deal with structural devices like paragraphs in nonfiction, poetic lines in poetry, linguistic markers in narrative stories, literature genres, Hebraisms, etc. Inherent within written literature we will find such languaging structures, but how will we interpret them? What meanings will we attribute to them?

OLD WORLD LITERARY DEVICES

When the ancients made scrolls in the preliterate times, they did not structure them with "Tables of Contents" as do modern books. Authors then never began their writings with any kind of prelude about what the reader would find in the text. In the place of such introductory material, at best, they might use a storytelling device to prelude their message. So many of the old manuscripts began with *a story* which would essentially *"outline" the book in terms of upcoming themes.* This would serve to prepare the reader by "seeding" thematic ideas that would come later.

For an example, consider Luke's opening story about Elizabeth and Mary and their songs of praise and celebration. These reflected *the "Hannah" story* of I Samuel, suggesting the theme of barrenness to fruitfulness, of the lowly raising to a new status, of the unsuspected, the surprise, etc. Within that story the author coded and preluded many of the gospel themes that he highlighted (Luke 1).

This illustrates just one of the differences between ancient and modern literary devices. Biblical literature gloried in *oral storytelling techniques*. Loaded throughout the texts we will find a great many oral literary devices which the authors would program into their writing in terms of word plays, plays on word sounds, repetitive phrases, etc. This illustrates also the importance of knowing the original languages.

THE SOCIO-POLITICAL CONTEXT AS CONTEXT

Hermeneutics preeminently direct the reader's mind to notice and take into account *the context* within which the writing occurs. This includes both the literary context of the material and the socio-historical context.

Imagine if you came across the following statement. How would you go about interpreting it? "King David's Watergate with Bathsheba became his downfall." Now all the linguistic and etymological work in the world on the word "Watergate" would not explain its significance. Without *the history* behind the Nixon Whitehouse years and his Presidency, "Watergate" would remain a hidden phrase. In fact, to break down the word and figure out how "water" and "gate" fits into the meaning completely misleads! In such a case, the sociological analysis behind the word comprises an essential component to *doing good hermeneutical work*. "Watergate" alludes to an event.

We call statements in literature that allude to events *allusional* statements. The value of this, in part, lies in the fact that it assists us in understanding how words work. For after all, linguistically, words serve merely as vehicles for conveying meaning. *Meaning (or semantics) does not reside in a word, but in the mind of the one attributing the meaning or significance.* What a "word" means therefore always depends on what the speaker or framer of that word intended it to mean. To discover that meaning, we have to discover the speaker, his or her world, the references to which they refer, etc. *We have to index.*

If meaning resided in the word itself, you could use some "authoritative" dictionary and settle the matter. But no dictionary exists as "the authoritative source" of meanings. Every dictionary merely relates the ways people current use words, how people have used words, the multiple meanings that people can give words in different contexts, and how such words came to carry such meanings. Dictionaries reflect usage, they do not create it. Nor do they regulate it as if they existed as some form of "word police."

Now when it comes to the New Testament (NT), you will find

allusional words and referents everywhere in the text. From Jesus' parables and apocalyptic statements, to Romans, Hebrews and Revelation, allusional statements predominate. In these writings, you will find God's call to Abraham (Gen. 12), the Egyptian exodus, the Sinai ordinance of the Torah by the hand of angels, the kingdom of David and Solomon, the Babylonian captivity, the restoration of Israel to their land, the Macabbean revolt, etc. Allusions to these events provided anecdotal prototypes.

So also with the events of AD 33. What happened when Jesus suffered crucifixion and death, resurrection and ascension, the beginning of the new kingdom on Pentecost, etc. all of these events became allusional events. Biblical writers used such terms and phrases as "the Cross," "Calvary," "Golgotha," "Christ's death," etc. These terms signify far more than their etymologies reveal. References to Christ's cross, death, or blood stood as *one word symbols* for both the events and their meanings. Theologians today speak about that entire context as "the Christ Event." We can subsume much theological significance by speaking about Good Friday, the Resurrection, sitting at the right hand of the majesty on high, etc.

The fall of Jerusalem in AD 70 also functions as such an event. The events of that year load up the term "A.D. 70" with much significance in terms of biblical covenant history. For in "the fall of Jerusalem" (AD 64-70) we can allude to Nero's persecution and madness, the Roman-Jewish War, the holocaust of Jerusalem, the end of theocratic Israel, the separation of Judaism and Christianity, the end of the apostolic age, the years of the great tribulation, the resurrection of the dead, etc. All of these allusions significantly impact one's understanding the new covenant as well as the writings that we call "the New Testament" scriptures. In fact, even if you don't buy the Preterist view presented herein, if you open the books of the NT without understanding **the historical milieu behind AD 70** in that first-century world, you would misunderstand many scriptures and theological ideas.

A clear understanding of the first century begins by realizing that Palestine existed as an enemy-occupied colony of Rome.

Consequently, by the sixth decade, the Zealot Movement in Palestine had become a formidable and explosive force that threatened Rome and endangered Israel. In AD 66, the seven-year Jewish-Rome War began with a fury that Josephus could only designate as a absolute and senseless "madness."

The first century milieu enables us to understand a little more about the politico-socio-grammatical-and religio-issues prevalent then. This hermeneutic context enables us to understand many of the biblical statements. *Historical milieu* plays an important role in the hermeneutic question. (A "milieu," from French, stands for an environment or setting.)

CONCLUSION

The literary milieu of the Bible reveals that we recognize the Bible as comprised of many different kinds of literature and writings. No wonder *understanding depends on the indexing process* (knowing who wrote it, when, to whom, why, about what, using what kind of literature, etc.). Texts always and inevitably become conditioned by their contexts. Rip a text apart from context and we create a pretext! If we make indiscriminate applications of the biblical text without taking into consideration the various levels of its context, we will more than likely impose our Western thought-patterns, beliefs, and presuppositions on the text. Not wise.

With regard to eschatology, all of this plays a crucial role. In this domain many use the biblical text with little precision and with lots of sloppy linguistics. They jump into exposition without indexing the text at all. They do a "cut and paste" kindergarten kind of theology that merely ties words from different texts together without checking context, etc. Such, in turn, creates a millennial madness that undermines the "sound mind" which God gives.

Chapter 2
**

INDEXING THE TIME ELEMENT

"When Did They Say the End would Occur?"
*"When Did They Predict
the Fulfillment of the 'at hand' Statements?"*

Suppose you got a letter out of your mailbox tomorrow. Opening it, you read, "I will arrive there soon and would like for us to go out for dinner during which time I have a business proposal that I would like to present to you something that I think you've waited for." From that reading would you get the impression from that author that he or she expected some important event to occur in the near future?

Suppose further that the author send a postcard the next week. "My coming is at hand." What would you think? Would you entertain the impression that you should expect this event wouldn't occur for thousands of years in the distant future? Of course not.

Suppose you felt that this event posed a great opportunity (or danger) to you? Would that create a sense of urgency? Suppose you trusted the author and totally believed that his writing represented something valid, authentic, and accurate. If he told that this highly significant event would occur "shortly," would you take that as a forthright communication about time?

This thought experiment precisely represents *the opening hermeneutic* (interpretation) *problem* that we discover in the writings of what we call "the New Testament" (NT). Consistently, all of the writers testify that *the end would occur "soon"* and *"at hand."* Together they concurred: it would occur "shortly." Now for people who want to take the Bible at its word and trust its inherent message, this poses a problem. **Did the eschatological events stand "at hand" or not?** If we interpret such propositional time-statements in non-literal ways, what else can we dismiss as figurative?

THE "AT HAND" END TIME APOCALYPTIC VISION

Because many (if not most) people do not realize just how pervasive this "soon" and "at hand" end-time message stands in the text of the NT, I think it expedient to take a good look at this. In order to get a sense of the predominance of this imminent "end of the world" message within the early Christians writings, notice the content, time element, and "felt sense" within the following quotations.

Reading these quotations will enable you to discover *the imminent end* message repeats constantly, consistently, and pervasively in the thought world of the NT writers. The predominance of awareness leaves us in no doubt that the apostles and early Christians lived in excited anticipation of the end of the old world and the beginning of the new.

All of the early writers expected the end to come in their day. As early as the 50s, Paul wrote them to "not to be quickly shaken in mind or excited, either by spirit or by word... to the effect that the day of the Lord has come" (II Thess. 2:2). He wrote to *slow down* their expectations of an imminent end. As he did, he also admitted that "the mystery of lawlessness" had **already** begun to work, yet there existed a restraining power temporarily holding it back.

When a few more years passed, Paul's temper became more urgent. To those at Rome, just prior to Nero's outbreak of madness and persecution in AD 64, he wrote,

> "The God of peace will **soon** crush 'satan' (antagonistic, opponent) under your feet" (Rom. 16:20).

The next year, writing to the Corinthians, Paul packaged some of his advice about Christian lifestyle as "Emergency Advice."

> "I think that in view of the impending distress it is well for a person to remain as he is.... Brethren, *the appointed time has grown very short;* from now on, let those who have wives live as though they had none...For the form of this world *is passing away"* (I Cor. 7:26, 29-31).

Nero's AD 64 horrible persecution affected not only Rome, but all outlying provinces. So Peter's epistles of the next year (65) warned those throughout Asia Minor about the coming "fiery ordeal" that would engulf them.

> *"The end of all things is at hand,* therefore keep sane and sober for your prayers" (I Pet. 4:7).

Judgment would begin at God's "house" (at the Temple in Jerusalem upon theocratic Israel), and "the same experience of suffering" required of some would be required of "your brotherhood throughout the world" (I Pet. 5:9). As the time got closer, Peter peppered his second epistle with traces of apocalyptic literature warning about the coming day of the Lord and the inevitable conflict believers would experience with the ungodly. Later that year Peter died by crucifixion while Paul died as Nero ordered him beheaded.

About that same time, an epistle to the Hebrew church in Jerusalem provided instructional warning about the vanishing of the old covenant (Heb. 8:13). Once they had suffered and had taken it joyfully (Heb. 10:34), but they had not yet resisted to the point of shedding their blood (12:4). That would come before long.

God would shake "the heavens and the earth" one more time and thereby usher in the eternal kingdom which "cannot be shaken" (Heb. 12:25-31). The Jewish-Christians now needed to "go outside the camp, bearing abuse for him" (13:13) as he had suffered outside the city. Judaism had become a "diverse and strange teaching; for it is well that the heart be strengthened by grace, not by foods" (13:9).

THE IMMINENT END OF THAT GENERATION
"This Generation Shall Not Pass Away Till..."

Jesus himself made several specific prophecies regarding the "end of the world." These clearly locate "the end" within the time frame of his generation--those people to whom he spoke and who existed as part of his original auditors.

> "Truly, I say to you that *this generation will not pass away till all these things take place"* (Matt. 24:34).

Here Jesus explicitly stated his expectation of a world-ending catastrophe within their lifetime. How much plainer could he have made himself? He specifically said that "some standing here" would not see death until they saw the coming of the kingdom and judgment at the end (Matt. 16:28).

Jesus' eschatological document that most completely expresses his thoughts about these matters we call *"The Little Apocalypse."* (You find it in the biblical text in Mark 13, Matthew 24, and Luke 21.) Herein Jesus predicted the end of an age. If you follow the "you" statements in those chapters, it becomes clear that he specifically addressed the people of his time. Exegetically, we cannot postpone these statements 1900 years before they find their referents.

Yet some try to postpone them. How do they do this? Fundamentalists like Hal Lindsey ("The Late Great Planet Earth," 1967) arbitrarily change the meaning of the word "generation." He simply asserts that it means "race." Hence, he interpreted Jesus as saying that the Jewish race would not pass away until all these things came to pass. Of course, making the shift in meaning of *"generation"* does not make any sense in the other places where Jesus used the word "generation" (see Matt. 1:1,17, Acts 13:36, Psalm 95:10-11// Heb. 3:10-11, Gen. 5:1, 15:14-15, Ex. 1:6).

How would "generation" as "race" hold up in Matthew 1 where Matthew asserted that there existed fourteen generations from Abraham to David? How does it make any sense that fourteen "races" existed between David to the deportation to Babylon? Or from that deportation to the Messiah? (Matt. 1:17). It does not.

Handling the scriptures in this way does not reflect sound scholarship at all, but a very sloppy handling of the text. Obviously, by *failing to index the word to the context* this approach created a distortion of a text. It created a distortion that we would otherwise experience as clear and precise. What causes this kind of mishandling of the text? People bring their theology and theological agendas to the text and read the text through these filters. This prevents an accurate exegesis of the text. They have made the hermeneutic device the question, "Does it fit and integrate with my theology?"

THE TEXT OF THE LITTLE APOCALYPSE
(**Matthew 24**)

Just prior to Jesus suffering betrayed and crucifixion, during the last days in Jerusalem at the feast, he made some statements about the temple that his disciples found utterly shocking. The last time he walked out of the temple, he commented, "Behold, your house is forsaken and desolate" (Matt. 23:38). His explanation? "All the righteous blood shed on the earth" (Palestine) would come upon "this generation" (Matt. 23:34-35,38).

His disciples didn't understand. So they responded. With incredulity "they pointed out to him the buildings of the temple" (Matt. 24:1). "They said, 'Look, Teacher, what wonderful stones and what wonderful buildings!'" (Mark 13:1). Luke added, "some spoke of the temple, how it was adorned with noble stones and offerings" (Luke 21:5).

What in Jesus' words elicited these responses? A core Hebrew presupposition. Namely, the Temple must exist in the glorious coming age of the Messiah. They reasoned, "No temple, no messianic age. The Messiah will reign from that Temple!" No wonder then that Jesus' words provoked their incredulity! They couldn't believe it.

To leave no ambiguity, Jesus amplified his words. He spoke about the desolation of the Temple. He used words so vividly clear that they terrified and confused his disciples.

> "As for these things which you see, the days will come when *there shall not be left here one stone upon another that will not be thrown down*" (Luke 21:6).

Well, that did it. Such words could only mean one thing to those literally minded disciples, "I'm talking about the end of the world!" So they framed their follow-up questions to address this:

> "Tell us, *when* will this be, and *what* will be the sign of your

> coming ('your presence, Greek: *parousia*) and of the close of the age ('world')?" (Matt. 24:2-3)

Ah! They sought to index Jesus' words as to when and where! They wanted to find out the specifics: when, where, what, how, etc.

Their perspective didn't allow for a forsaken temple as part of their eschatology expectations. For them, the messianic kingdom could not come without the temple. They also thought that the temple would always stand. They couldn't err about that, could they? As a prerequisite for the Messiah, it had to remain. No temple = no messiah. Conceptually the idea of a forsaken temple, destroyed temple blew them away!

"There will not be left here *one stone upon another* which will not be thrown down!" describes a dismantling of the Temple which could only mean--*the end of the world!* The world of the Jewish Theocracy with the Messiah reigning from Jerusalem would also disappear.

In answering these questions in his Olive Apocalypse, Jesus put *a time frame around* the overall context of "the end." Note his concluding words, "In truth, I tell you, this generation (Greek: genea) will by no means pass away until all of these things take place" (Matt. 24:34). *He thereby time-dated* all of the preceding phenomenon. The end of the favored place of Israel and of Israel theocracy would occur in that generation. It would occur when someone, somehow, at some time, etc. would dismantle the Temple stone by stone. Jesus' thoughts regarding this world-changing saga portrayed them as continuing through the period of a generation.

> "When you see Jerusalem *surrounded with armies*, then you will know that the desolation of it has drawn near" (Luke 21:20).

Luke's "armies" replaces Matthew's Hebraic phrase *"the abomination of desolation."* This provides us a major clue about to how to understand and interpret this Hebraic apocalyptism, does it not? Luke's translation means that the Roman armies would consist of the desolating sacrilege of the great tribulation that would bring the end. Those armies would comprise the ones who would bring the tribulation and serve as God's punishing instrument for that judgment day.

Before this end, Jesus said there would arise a time of persecution and "great tribulation" which would come upon Israel. He said that Jews and Romans would haul his disciples into courts and tribunals, that all nations would hate them for his sake, that they would betray one another, that a falling away would occur, that false prophets would arise, and there would come a great suffering (e.g. Matthew 24:9-24, Luke 21:10-19). Upon presenting these signs of the times, Jesus explained, "Lo, I have told you beforehand. ... So also, when you see all these things, you know that he is near, at the very gates" (Matt. 24:25,33).

THE INTERPRETATION STRUGGLE
The Schools of Interpretative Thought

How should we understand these words of an imminent end? What specifically did Jesus and his apostles think concerning the time frame of the coming of the kingdom, the end of the world, and the beginning of another? Did they turn out accurate or wrong? If not literally, then in what other way could one world have ended and another begun? Did they speak literally, spiritually, covenantally, or figuratively?

Without question, these documents provide a powerful sense that they expected some major event or events to come to a completion *very "soon."* The words "at hand," "soon," "within this generation," etc. provide too clear and direct a message to think otherwise. They also occur too frequently to dismiss them as some trivial mistake that crept into the text.

Liberal scholarship has more honestly reckoned with the urgency theme of immediacy. H. J. Schoeps (1961) wrote,

> "We should misunderstand the apostle's letters as a whole, and the governing consciousness from which they sprang, if we failed to recognize that Paul only lives, writes, and preaches, in the unshakable conviction that his generation represents the last generation of mankind" (*Paul, The Theology of the Apostle in the Light of Jewish Religious History*).

But the liberal scholars tend to dismiss the immediacy factor as simply *a mistaken or delusional idea* of the apostles.

> "Jesus and the early writers were simply mistaken because they simply became caught up with the spirit of Jewish apocalyptism of the time."

In his book, *"The Quest of the Historical Jesus,"* Albert Schweitzer (1961) wrote,

> "The whole history of 'Christianity' down to the present day...is based on the delay of the Parousia, the non-occurrence of the Parousia, the abandonment of eschatology, the progress and completion of the 'de-eschatologising' of religion which has been connected therewith."

In writing this way *Schweitzer simply began with the assumption* that the parousia and end did not occur. Another liberal scholar, Rudolf Bultmann (1957), wrote,

> "The problem of Eschatology grew out of the fact that *the expected end of the world failed to arrive*, that the 'Son of man' did not appear in the clouds of heaven, that history went on, and that the eschatological community could not fail to recognize that it had become a historical phenomenon and that the Christian faith had taken on the shape of a new religion." (*History and Eschatology: the Presence of Eternity*).

This statement demonstrates his working presuppositions. He assumed that "the end of the world" would come literally and would end "history." But as we will see, that perspective does not reflect the Hebraic perspective of apocalyptic literature. Max King (1987) noted that Bultmann assumed that *history* (and human history at that) existed as the subject of the Bible's eschatology rather than *Israel* (who existed as God's creation for the purposes of redemption) (*The Cross and the Parousia of Christ*).

Accepting the text for what it says and concluding that "the end" of the biblical writers did not occur lead the field of liberal scholars into assuming that neither the text nor the word of Jesus and his followers hold true, valid, or accurate.

Assuming (erroneously) along with others that "the end" referred to mankind, to history, to planet earth, they could conclude nothing other than it simply did not happen. This consequently lead them to hold a "lower" view of inspiration; that the biblical text contains lots of errors --common human errors of understanding, perspective, etc.

On the other side of the spectrum we find those scholars who accept the "higher" view of inspiration, namely, that the biblical text demonstrates accuracy, truth, and insights not discoverable by human reasoning. They contest the accusation that the text suffers many errors. So *conservative scholars* have struggled to figure out a way for the biblical text to maintain its truthfulness (in making statements about an eminent end) and their perception that the end did not happen.

Consequently, as they have handled this difficulty of the literal time-language ("the end is near"), some invented the supposed "postponement" theory. They assert that Jesus and his apostles accurately announced that the end "is at hand," but he then postponed the coming, the fullness of the kingdom, the end, etc. because that generation of the Jewish nation did not accept him.

When these people read the imminent language of the end of the world, they admit that Jesus and his apostles did expect a soon coming end as did the early Christians. But because they take the apocalyptic language of *Revelation* literally (except for Chapter 1 and verse 1!), they can't figure out how it could have already occurred. This begins their dilemma. Yet this dilemma deepens since they refuse to attribute this failure of the events to occur as a mistaken notion of the writers, or an error in the apostles. What would that do to their high view of biblical inspiration?

Thus rose this *invention*--the doctrine of postponement. This theological theory goes something like this. "When the Jews rejected Jesus, his apostles and their message of the kingdom, Jesus postponed the kingdom and the end of the age. It will all happen, but at some later date." From this beginning assumption, many other interpreters have built elaborate theories of premillennialism and dispensationalism.

When we step back from both the liberal and conservative interpretative schemes, it becomes obvious that *both feel the power and impact of the time urgency statements* in the NT writings. Both hermeneutic systems seek to deal with, or get rid of, the impact of this "at hand-ness." The one thing that unites both liberal and conservative interpretations lies in their working **assumption**, namely, "the end of the world" did not occur because it did not come literally. And because it did not end history or the planet, they jump to the conclusion that the world did not come to an end, the apocalyptic has not yet occurred.

The liberal perspective leads its adherents to the conclusion that the poor uneducated first-century writers suffered from a pathetic misguidance and confusion. "They simple state a error about the time element." For these thinkers, biblical inspiration did not protect the original writers from such errors. The conservative perspective leads its adherents to devising theologies to "explain," rationalize, and distort their words in order to avoid the strength of the immediacy.

THE CHALLENGE
THAT TRANSFORMED MY THINKING

Years ago, I was studying and teaching *Revelation* using the traditional assumptions about *Revelation's* late date (AD 96). A close friend, David Rossiter, asked me some hard questions that got me thinking and challenged my own presuppositions. "*Why* do you take the repeated statements in *Revelation* about the "time being at hand," "soon," "shortly," etc. and apply them to events that would not occur for a hundred, two hundred, or three hundred years?"

I answered weakly, "It represents the closest fulfillment I can find." Beginning with that late date, I assumed that John's "*Apocalypse*" referred to the Roman persecution of the Christians in the second and third centuries. Yet I felt the strain of applying *Revelation* to a judgment against the Roman Empire that didn't occur until AD 476--not exactly "soon!"

David then asked *the question* that began unsettling all my presuppositions. "What specifically *within* the *Apocalypse* itself demands the late AD 96 date?" If he had asked where I received my ideas about that date for *Revelation*, or upon what basis did I opt for the late dating of *Revelation*, I could have quoted the traditional arguments one can find in any commentary. That would not have shaken me so. I could have given him that data without any problem. But when he asked about "What within the text of *Revelation* itself" lead me to the late date, that posed an entirely different question.

At that moment, I didn't know. I had no answer for that one. I mumbled, "The 7 heads represent the 7 hills of Rome." But I could feel the flimsiness of that answer. I also had some other scriptures from the text of *Revelation* flying furiously through my mind which I knew suggested an early date rather than a late one like that standing, existing Temple of Ch. 11.

Not knowing what a profound effect his question would eventually have upon me, David continued. "*What if* everything in *Revelation* referred to the Jewish holocaust of AD 70? What if the great persecution that brought an end to Paul and Peter, that decimated the Jewish race, land, temple, religion, etc. stood as the referents for the Sea and Land Beasts?"

Well those questions initiated a new study for me. I immediately sat down and read the entire *Apocalypse* from the perspective that it existed as *an oracle of the end of the Jewish world*. Suddenly the lights came on. Now the Jewishness of *Revelation* made perfect sense. "Yes, it makes sense to complete biblical revelation with 'the end' of the fleshly theocratic nation, so that the new spiritual Israel could arise and become the bearer of the new covenant. No wonder John overload it with OT allusions and references! He wrote it to the Hebrew believers. He wrote it about *the end of their old covenant world.*"

Using this new frame-of-reference, from the perspective of a Hebrew-Christian in the first century, completely shifted my thinking about many other sayings and prophecies in the NT writings. I should not have found this a new frame of reference since the majority of NT documents addressed precisely this same audience, the early Hebrew-Christians.

COULD ALL OF THE "NEW TESTAMENT" WRITINGS COMPRISE A PRE-AD 70 VOLUME?

As I began researching these questions, I came upon the works of the liberal New Testament scholar, John A. T. Robertson. In particular his book, *"Redating The New Testament"* struck me with an usual force. In this work Robertson explored a particular problem of the first century.

> "One of the oddest facts about the NT is that... *the single most datable and climactic event of the period--the fall of Jerusalem in AD 70,* and with it the collapse of institutional Judaism based on the temple is never once mentioned *as a past fact."*

Amazing!

Robertson asked himself, "Just *why* any of the books of the NT needed to be put after the fall of Jerusalem. He said he felt it exceptionally "strange that this cataclysmic event was never once mentioned or apparently hinted at." "So, as little more than a theological joke, I thought I would see how far one could get with *the hypothesis that the whole of the NT was written before 70."*

His work, *"Redating The New Testament,"* grew from this research question. In this work he more fully developed his hypothesis that all of the books within the NT writings existed prior to the AD 70 event. Subsequently, I did my own research to see how far I could get with the same hypothesis. The further I went, the more I also felt compelled by the facts to limit all of the canonical books to pre-AD 70 dates. I could find no compelling evidence for doing otherwise. Can you?

One fact that I found intriguing and convincing arose from a contrast with other books of that era. Nearly every document written after AD 70, both Jewish and Christian (of which many exist) refer to the destruction of Jerusalem. Yet not one document in the NT mentioned it *as a past event*. Robinson calls this "an arresting fact." And indeed it certainly should arrest our attention. For it strongly implies that every book in our NT canon must have existed before AD 70. This marvel would exist on the order of a current historical writing about the 20th. century Europe that never mentioned the holocaust of World War II.

COMPARING THE NT SCRIPTURES
WITH DOCUMENTS THAT CAME AFTER AD 70

If nearly all of the literature among the Jews and Christians after

AD 70 referenced the Fall of Jerusalem, does that make it incredible that there exists not one such reference in the NT? How should we interpret this?

II Baruch clearly reflects the fall of Jerusalem although it purports to exist as an announcement of the prophet Baruch of coming Chaldean invasion. This functions as an after the event prophecy from an uninspired someone. "We have overthrown the wall of Zion and we have burnt the palace of the mighty God" (7:1). "They delivered... to the enemy the overthrown wall, and plundered the house, and burned the temple" (80.3).

The Sibylline Oracles: "And a Roman leader shall come to Syria, who shall burn down Solyma's (Jerusalem's) Temple with fire, and therewith slay many men, and shall waste the great land of the Jews with its broad way" (41:25-27).

Barnabas: "Because they (the Jews) went to war, it (the Temple) was pulled down by their enemies" (16:4). Look at the explicitness of that statement--precisely the kind of statement so conspicuously absent from the NT.

I Baruch, generally dated AD 75, takes the form of a story that the author frames as told in the year BC 586. This however operates as a thin disguise for the Romans in AD 70. In the book it tells about parents eating children (2:3); the burning of the city (1:2); the deportation of the captives to Rome (4:6,15ff,31ff, 5:6)--events that transpired in AD 70. "After a little interval Zion will again be builded, and its offerings will again be restored, and the priests will return to their ministry, and also the Gentiles will come to glorify it. Nevertheless, not fully as in the beginning" (68:5ff).

Apocalypse of Abraham. "I looked and saw; Lo! the picture swayed and from it emerged, on the left side, a heathen people, and these pillaged those who were on the right side, men and women and children: some they slaughtered, others they retained with themselves. Lo! I saw them run towards them through four entrances, and they burned the Temple with fire, and the holy things that were therein they plundered."

II Esdras. "You see how our Sanctuary has been laid waste, our alter demolished, and our Temple destroyed. Our harps are unstrung, our hymns silenced, our shouts of joy cut short; the light of the sacred lamp is out, and the ark of the covenant has been taken as spoil; the holy vessels are defiled, and the name which God has conferred on us is disgraced; our leading men have been treated shamefully, our priests burned alive, and the Levites taken off into captivity; our virgins have been raped, and our wives ravished, our Godfearing men carried off, and our children abandoned, our youths have been enslaved, and our strong warriors reduced to weakness. Worst of all Zion, once sealed with God's own seal, has forfeited its glory and is in the hands of our enemies" (10:21-23).

The Didache has come down to us with a very early date, very early, AD 40 to 60. In notable distinction from *Barnabas*, the Jewish Apocalypses of *Baruch* and *II Esdras*--no hint exists in it of any such event lying in the past or future.

I Clement, dated as written in the early months of AD 70 before the catastrophe occurred. According to I Clement, the Jewish priests continued to that day offering the daily sacrifices (41:2); and the Neronian persecution existed as very fresh in his memory (5:1--6:2).

These kinds of statements stand out in all post AD 70 documents and yet we find them glaringly missing from the NT. It makes sense that so much of the literature in Judaism and Christianity after AD 70 attempted to come to terms with that catastrophe. Accordingly, to assume that Jewish and Christian authors would have written without reference to such a cataclysmic event pushes our credulity to the limits. We can only conclude the high improbability of such a hypothesis.

ADDITIONAL TIME CONSTRAINT VERSES

In contrasting the old and new covenants by comparing "angels" and Jesus, the Hebrew writer asks, "Are they not all ministering spirits sent forth to serve, for the sake of those who are to obtain salvation?" (1:14). Other translations read, "because of the ones *being about to inherit salvation."* Here the author suggests that something in the immediate future will bring some coming "salvation."

Later, the same writer used the present tense (writing in AD 65-66), "He [Jesus] abolishes the first in order to establish the second" (Heb. 10:9). The KJV records, "that he may establish the second." This does not say that he "took away" (past tense) the first. It refers to something yet future!

Then, later in that same chapter, the writer said, "For yet a little while, and the coming one shall come and *shall not tarry...*" (Heb. 10:37). The NAS version says *he "will not delay."* Yet if the second coming has not yet occurred, that would represent quite a delay--a delay that has now extended some two-thousand years.

Finally, Don K. Preston (1994) has noted the use of these terms of imminence. Regard "near," he contrasted it with Balaam's statement that the Redeemer he saw in his prophet vision "was 'far off' and 'not near'" (Numbers 24:17ff). "Near" as a temporal statement refers to something close at hand.

CONCLUSION

The time question explores *when* Jesus and his disciples thought "the end" would occur. With this crucial question we must ask contextual and historical questions about **what** those people expected. To understanding any piece of literature we need to know *the temporal context* of the writing and what temporal (time) language the author used.

Those who do not believe that Jesus and his disciples taught and expected that the end would come soon must address these **time statements** regarding the temporal phrases used throughout their writings that refer to "the end" being close, near, at hand, upon them, etc.

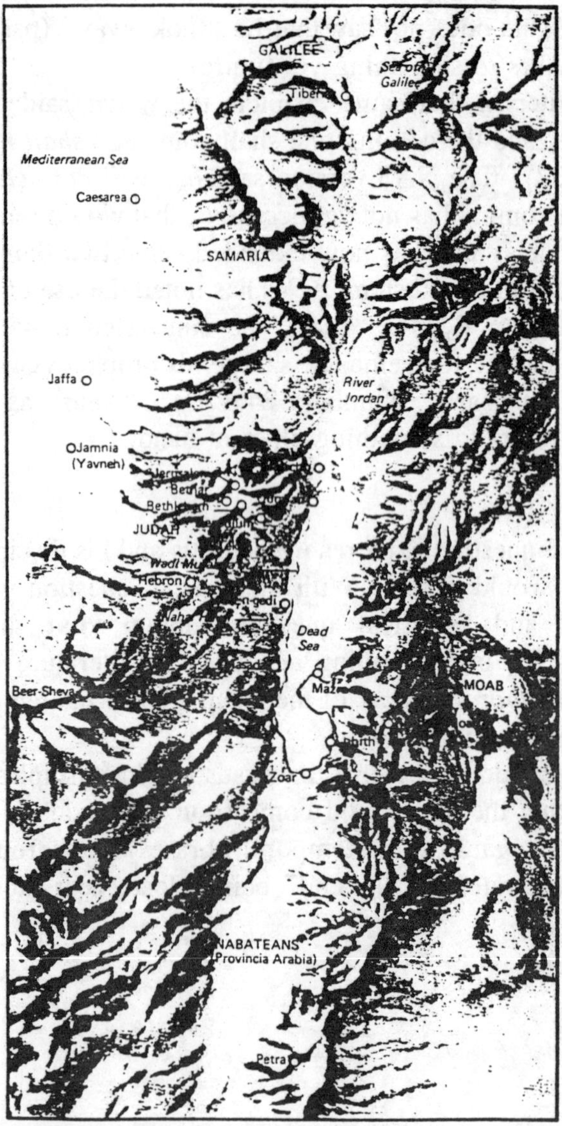

GALILEE
Mediterranean Sea
Caesarea
SAMARIA
Jaffa
River Jordan
Jamnia (Yavneh)
JUDAH
Hebron
Dead Sea
Beer-Sheva
MOAB
Zoar
NABATEANS (Provincia Arabia)
Petra

Chapter 3
**

INDEXING WHERE

*"Where and Under What Conditions
Did The Apostles Speak of The End?"*

How much do you know about the socio-political and religious situation that characterized Israel in the first century? How much do you know about the growing antagonism between Jew and Christian that developed in the years following Pentecost until the outbreak of the Jewish-Roman War in AD 66?

What socio-political understandings do you have about some of the events that transpired in the book of *"the Acts of the Apostles"* as the Zealot Jews and Pharisees chased and persecuted Paul from city to city in Asia Minor, and then as the Roman Guard in Jerusalem arrested him on the steps of the Temple after the Jewish mob outcry due to a misunderstanding (Acts 21)?

Without understanding *the current events* of the day and age when the NT writings and prophecies arose, *how can one make an informed judgment* whether "the signs of the times" that Jesus spoke about in his Olivet Apocalypse (Matthew 24, Mark 13, Luke 21) came to pass in that generation, or not? I ask that question rhetorically. Obviously we cannot!

Without knowing the situation of those times, without knowing the religious and political situation of that day, without knowing the mental-emotional and psychological background of the writers and recipients--a person would not have *the necessary facts* to call his or her judgments "informed." (And we know what we call people who jump the gun and make "uninformed judgments, don't we?) People who rush in without the appropriate and necessary facts about things act "ignorantly" (without information), others act/talk "stupidly" (don't use the intelligence they do have). Intelligence and wisdom move us to get the facts before making judgments.

If you want to hold an informed opinion on some matter, you need to know some facts. Pathetically, you can turn on television and radio almost any day of the week and hear many current interpreters and speakers about "end time things" who do not even know some of the basic facts about *the context of the early Christians*.

They seem ignorant of basic biblical information regarding the early Hebrew Christian church:

- that no Gentiles existed in that church from 30 to 42,
- that the Palestinian-Zionistic branch responded with lots of prejudice and racism when the Gentiles begin to enter the church (Acts 10-15),
- that James, Peter and Paul along with the elders at Jerusalem had to convene a council at Jerusalem to calm down the Pharisee fundamentalists in the church (Acts 15:5),
- that a nationalistic Zionistic movement arose in the sixth decade,
- that the Jewish-Roman war broke out in AD 66 and continued for seven horrifying years,
- that a terrible holocaust of great tribulation came upon Israel which climaxed in the fall of Jerusalem in AD 70, etc.

This information plays a crucial role for anyone who wants to make intelligent evaluations about the biblical text. Without such information, we think and talk "in the dark" (mentally) about *the social, historical, religious context* within which the authors wrote their epistles and documents, and the possible events to which they referred.

THE "JEWISH" PROBLEM IN THE EARLY CHURCH

To fully appreciate the NT letters, and the historical account of the early Christian movement in *Acts*, we need to begin by attempting to understand the relationship between the faithful Hebrew community and those messianic Jews who gave their allegiance to the Nazareth prophet. This distinction contrasts those orthodox Jews and those Jews who increasingly became more and more unorthodox because they believed and gave their allegiance to Jesus as the Messiah.

At first, during the days immediately following Pentecost, the Jews of the new faith "found favor with all the people" (Acts 2:47). In fact, they continued to worship at the Temple and maintain all of their old Jewish heritage. They didn't see that such would conflict with their new allegiance. *The new covenant Christian faith began essentially as a Jewish phenomenon* (Acts 2-3). As far as these early Hebrew believers felt, their affirmation of faith in Christ did not negate their Jewish experience at all. For them, it fulfilled it. Today we might call them "fulfilled Jews."

This attitude continued to prevail in the thinking of the Hebrew Church in Jerusalem thirty years later. In AD 59, Paul returned to Jerusalem with funds for those in need who had suffered from the famine. Jesus' physical brother, James, served as the central pastoral figure in that church. In his thinking and living, he adopted a style fully Hebrew. This James, as one of the key pillars of that mother church, enjoyed popular acclaim *among the Jews* as "James the Just."

When Paul came to James, James warned Paul.

> "You see, brother, how many thousands there are among the Jews of those who have believed; they are all *zealous for the law*" (Acts 21:20).

Not only did they still (30 years after Pentecost) *see themselves as law-zealous Jews,* but even more crucially, they held Paul in great suspicion. "They have been told about you that you teach all the Jews who are among the Gentiles to forsake Moses, telling them not to circumcise their children or observe the customs" (Acts 21:21).

These comprised "fighting words" in those days. Those early Christians simply would not tolerate some supposed church leader like Paul out in the Roman world downplaying Moses, Jewish customs, or the Temple. How dare he! Those early believers did not share our respect for Paul. And given the rising Jewish nationalism, they reacted to Paul as if to a heretic!

To alleviate these fears, James told Paul to go to the Temple, take a Hebrew vow upon himself, go through purification according to the Torah, and show the zealot Hebrew Christians that they had nothing to worry about (Acts 21:22-24). "Thus all will know that there is nothing in what they have been told about you, but *that you yourself live in observance of the law*" (21:24).

What do we have here? Paul--a practicing Jew!? Don't you find that absolutely amazing? Here in the bosom of the mother Church existed ten-thousands of thousands of messianic Jews who believed in Jesus as Messiah and yet who also still believed the Old Testament Torah comprised the heart of Christian reality. No wonder they felt "zealous for the law!" No wonder early Christianity had such a difficult time getting away from the Judaistic influences! Separating from that Hebraic devotion to the Torah did not occur overnight. The complete transition from the old covenant to the new took both *a slow evolutionary process and a revolutionary process* (the AD 70 holocaust).

No wonder the early Gentile Christians outside of Jerusalem, and some Jews like Paul, had *a "Jewish problem."* The "Jewish" problem arose because, on the one hand, "salvation was of the Jews" (John 4:22), and on the other hand, salvation left Judaism to transcend it. The new faith stayed highly wedded to Judaism during the first forty years. Then those who began to catch a vision of God's Abrahamic plan ("to bless all nations") began to find the womb of Judaism suffocating. The Jewish Torah consisted of the school-master (custodian) to bring men to Christ (Gal. 3:19). Yet God had designed it to eventuate in a universal faith transcending "Jew and Greek" (Gal. 3:28). Yet the transition to that point took a long while and much trouble.

The ploy by James and Paul ultimately did not work. Accusations from some "Jews from Asia" flew hot and heavy against Paul. On the seventh day, they spotted Paul and "stirred up all the crowd and laid hands on him." "Men of Israel, help!

This is the man who is teaching men everywhere against the people and the law and this place; moreover he also brought Greeks into the Temple, and he has defiled this holy place." (Acts 21:27-28). This comprised the misunderstanding that landed Paul in prison.

Thereafter the Romans sent Paul to prison, first in Jerusalem (Acts 21-24), then in Caesarea (Acts 25:6), and finally in Rome (Acts 27-28). During those years (59 to 64) Paul defended himself repeatedly *against the accusations of the theocratic Jews and the Judaistic believers.* He argued that his experience in chains existed "for hope in **the promise** made by God **to our fathers**..." And from those prisons, he wrote what we now call his prison epistles.

THE SOCIO-POLITICO-RELIGIOUS TRANSITION FROM JUDAISM TO CHRISTIANITY

Though the new covenant came to "the Jews first" on Pentecost and the messianic Jews (or early Christians) "found favor with all the people" (Acts 2:47), the favorable PR didn't last. Soon afterwards the Jewish leaders (the Sanhedrin) still reeling from the events of Jesus' crucifixion, began to come down hard on some of the apostles (Acts 3-4). Hoping that the Jesus-mania would eventually die down, they attempted to leave them alone.

When, however, the new covenant people accepted the Hellenistic Jews into the Church (Acts 6), things began to change. This brought about a growing influence of Hellenistic ideas which culminated in *Stephen's radical "Anti-Temple" message* (Acts 6:13-14, Acts 7). And that, in turn, lead to his trial and martyrdom before the Sanhedrin.

With Stephen's death, and the liberalizing influence of the church welcoming Hellenistic Jews, *there arose "a great persecution" against those of the way.* It "arose against the church in Jerusalem" and caused all to become scattered throughout the region, "except the apostles" (Acts 8:1).

As you think about that, doesn't it strike you as strange? The Jews could live with and tolerably accept the Messianic-Jews

(Christian), but not if they became radical about liberalizing the Hebrew faith and, in particular, in adopting *an anti-Temple mentality*. Sadly, the rejection and expulsion of the Hellenists from Jerusalem, in turn, made the mother church even more conservative. As the liberal segments went elsewhere, the Hebrew Church took on more and more of the characteristics of *the Palestinian Zionist movement*. Later, this would serve to their detriment and explain why so many of them perished in the fall of Jerusalem.

The "Jewish Problem" eventually came to a breaking point for the church as the more liberal segment of the church caught the vision of the new Temple consisting of the lives of the believers rather than the old physical Temple of Solomon. The Hellenistic believers, while Jewish in race, adopted more and more of the Greek culture in their manner and way of life.

This explains why the apostles remained unmolested in Jerusalem (Acts 8:1). The orthodox Jews tolerated them since they looked Hebrew, thought Hebraically, and valued things Hebraic. They served as no threat to their way of life. The Hellenists, however, with their liberalizing tendencies caused them to not look Hebrew, not think Hebrew enough, and not value the old Hebrew ways. The Jews fairly well tolerated the Hebrew Christians for awhile because they maintained their Hebraic culture. You can see this tolerance during the time of James' leadership in Jerusalem until his death in AD 62. It continued until the time when the Roman/Jewish War broke out (66 AD).

In Israel, the Palestinian Christians had neither the desire nor the courage to take the daring steps of their more liberal brethren. Paul, who became one of the "liberals," caught a vision of *the universality of the new covenant*. But he had to go to Antioch to pursue that vision. There the more liberal branch of the movement felt moved to push out even further--to the very Gentiles (Acts 13:1-3).

This very action of taking the good-news to the entire Greek/Roman world, without first proselytizing them as Jewish converts, greatly offended the Jerusalem church. The faithful fundamental Hebrew Christians couldn't believe the brashness of that move! Accordingly, the Palestinian Christians confronted Paul and his team about their right to do this and about the very basis whereby a person could claim the name of Christ. This showdown occurred at the Jerusalem Conference of Acts 15.

Now, true enough, the early Hebrew Christians believed they consisted of *the true eschatological remnant of Israel.* In Palestine, some even called them "Nazarenes," because they kept the law. Even Peter, more than ten years after Pentecost, still declared the he had never eaten any "unclean" food (Acts 10:14)! Don't you find that amazing? Talk about maintaining himself and his lifestyle as a true Jew after ten years of the new covenant! Luke described Ananias, who laid hands on Saul, as "highly respected by all the Jews" living in Damascus (Acts 22:12).

Conversely, Luke tells about the Hellenist Philip who clearly disregarded the Torah when he baptized the Ethiopian eunuch (Acts 8:22-39). That violated one of the tenants of Judaism (Deut. 23:1). But the biggest, and most radical, change occurred approximately ten or so years after Pentecost with the acceptance of *actual Gentiles* into the faith--without them first becoming Jewish proselytes.

In that instance, the Jerusalem elders and the other apostles called Peter on the carpet. They demanded that he give account of himself to the Jerusalem counsel (Acts 11). During that time *"the circumcision party criticized him..."* (Acts 11:2). The who? The conservative, fundamental Pharisee believers (Acts 15:5). They comprised the ones who engaged Paul and Barnabas with "no small dissension and debate" (Acts 15:2).

All this means that *the Christian revolution* did not begin at Pentecost with a clear vision of the ecumenicity of the gospel. No! Though Peter unknowingly hinted at it (Acts 2:39), it would take more than a decade before the idea of the trans-Jewish gospel would take seed. The Christian movement only evolved slowly toward its ultimate goal of becoming a blessing "to all nations." The ecumenicity didn't begin in earnest until the church at Antioch decided to begin Christian missions to "all the world" (Acts

11:19-30, 13:1ff).

Now in your mind skip two decades to the time of the Zealot Revolution in the sixth decade of the first century and you suddenly discover a Judaism that no longer tolerated the messianic-Jews. The missions to the Gentiles has intensified the antagonistic feelings between the early believers and Judaism.

Accordingly, the unbelieving Zionistic Jews throughout the Empire became *the major antagonistic force* to Paul and his evangelistic team. In *Acts*, "the Jews" chased, persecuted, arrested, imprisoned, and tortured Paul everywhere he went on his trips. They forever accused, blasphemed, and stirred up the synagogue leaders against him as a heretic. As the years passed their insane jealousy and cruelty increased, so did Paul's words. With stronger and stronger language, he eventually called them "dogs," "evil-workers," "mutilators of the flesh" (Phil. 3:2).

The days of mutual peace, cooperation, and tolerance ended. Raised in the womb of Judaism, Christianity began experiencing *the beginning of the birth-pangs* (Romans 8:18-25) that would eventually totally separate it from the source of its birth. The children of Abraham by faith would become separated from the children of Abraham by blood (Gal. 3-4).

Accordingly, *a forty-year transition period* occurred wherein the old fleshly disbelieving Judaism increasingly disbelieved and degenerated. It degenerated further and further into a demonic thing as it became more and more engulfed by the "satanic" notions of the nationalistic, Zionistic movement. The more they gave themselves to the idea that, "We have Abraham as our father!" the more they became the target of God's coming wrath. "Even now the ax is laid to the root of the trees..." (Matt. 3:7-10). This *nationalistic Judaism* functioned as one of the antichrists about which Peter, Jude, Paul, and John wrote such stringent words (I John 2:17-18, 4:1-4).

Nationalistic-Zionistic Judaism then consisted of the *"sitz em leben"* of the conflict that challenged those early believers in the first century. Further, by recognizing that the writing of the NT canon ended by AD 70, we clearly identify **the central problem** facing the early churches. **Judaism!** Gnosticism did not consist of the main problem, but a degenerate Judaism that had forgotten their vision and who had become so unbelieving that a great many of them did not give their allegiance to their own Jewish Messiah. Until AD 70 the main problem, in the relation between the new faith of the Messiah and the old heritage of the Hebrew people, consisted of the Jewish theocratic national itself. It became a "satan" (opponent) to the spiritual believers who accepted God's messiah.

The early Jewish problem concerned the role of the Torah, the Temple, the priesthood, the Hebrew way of life, and the Hebrew people as the theocratic nation given to introduce to the gentile world *the new covenant.* To this issue, Paul devoted three full chapters in his Roman letter (Romans 9-11, see Ch. 5) while the writer to the "Hebrews" devoted his entire epistle (see Ch. 6).

What point did Paul make in those writings? Primarily that *God's covenant promise to Abraham* (to "bless all nations") came from, within, and through **Israel** (in the person of Jesus of Nazareth). This means that *the hope of Israel* consisted of an ecumenical hope from the beginning. Now anyone (everyone) could access it--if they believed (Rom. 10:12-13). Now God offered it, no longer on the basis of nation or race, *en masse*, to anyone--not even to Israel. He had started a process for replacing the old covenant and, indeed, that old in AD 64 had become "ready to vanish away" (Heb. 8:13) as the "new Jerusalem" (the church) would replace the old arrangement.

WHEN JUDAISM BECAME HERETICAL & DEMONIC

In those transitional forty years the movement of "the Way" struggled against Judaism, not Gnosticism. So in the epistles of Romans, Galatians, and Colossians, the problem the author addressed concerned *traditional and Zionistic Judaism.*

In the pastoral epistles (Timothy and Titus), the General letters (II Peter and Jude), and the Johannian literature (John, the three letters, and Revelation)--this "Jewish" problem had grown to become one of a much more serious nature. The Jewish problem portrayed in these works had become *immoral, ascetic, and demonic*. Now "the Jews" (unbelieving Israel who rejected the messiah) belonged to "the world." And by AD 68, they had become the "synagogue of Satan" (Rev. 3:9). Strong language, wouldn't you say?

This reveals the full development of the Judaistic problem as it spanned the years. During the forty years of the interface between the old and new, the new faith went from "finding favor with all the people," worshipping with them in the Temple, to becoming a degenerated and demonic Zionistic racism by the time of the Zealot Revolution in the 60s. No wonder Peter, Jude, Paul, John and the fourth gospel spoke so harshly of it.

As "the synagogue of Satan," Judaism, the very mother and cradle of Christianity, became more and more of an *"antagonistic and oppositional force"* (hence the literal meaning of the word "satan") to the church. As Peter became a "satan" to Jesus when he refused to accept Jesus' dying and rising again (Matt. 16:21-24), so the woman that gave birth to "the man child who would rule the nations" became the harlot woman of the apocalypse (Rev. 12, 17).

THEN CAME THE APOCALYPTIC TIMES OF "THE END" OF ISRAEL

In the first century, the decade of the sixties functioned as the "times that tried the souls of men." During those years, the "signs of the times" that Jesus foretold began to occur. Various socio-political events began to transpire that ultimately led to the Roman-Jewish War, the great tribulation within that conflict, the siege and final fall of Jerusalem, the end to Israel as God's one and only theocratic nation, the holocaust of the Jewish nation, etc. All these things began to occur before the generation Jesus spoke to as he promised (Matthew 24).

In order to empower the believers to respond to those apocalyptic times, the apostles and disciples of Jesus began writing numerous documents (gospels, epistles, pastorals, and apocalypses) which later church fathers of the second and third century put together and labeled "the New Testament." (Actually this mislabeling has created much misunderstanding about the nature of the new covenant, for God does not write his new covenant with ink on paper or with fire in stone, but on living hearts with his spirit, II Cor. 3:3-6.)

Now some of these apostolic manuscripts aimed to conserve things as the believers went into the storm (the Pastorals). Others provide information for the storm itself--to brace up the Christians for the coming apocalyptic times (e.g. Revelation, I Peter, I Corinthians, etc.).

The significance of this insight reveals that the authors wrote the epistles and other documents not as theological treatises or scholarly tomes for posterity. They wrote them within *a socio-political context of grave danger,* and so we should read them in that light. Without so contextualizing the books to the religious, political, social, and cultural context out of which they came, we could very easily assume and treat these works as calm theological treatises on the philosophy of religion. Yet to do so would create a major cause of misunderstanding.

The apostolic writings do **not** represent theological dissertations. Read them. They sound more like marching orders! Do they not address living-the-faith issues about a world ready to fall apart? Do they not sound more like tracks for coping? And as emergency literature for hanging tough?

Understanding these events with their historical and political background enables us to *recapture the perspective* that the original writers used when speaking about them theologically and spiritually. For them, the fall of Jerusalem and the Jewish National state comprised "the end of the world" which had to occur so *the new world of the gospel* (what we call "the Christian age") could come in its fullness. This historical perspective regarding the context of that world enables us to adjust our understanding to many things that otherwise we would find confusing in the NT text.

No wonder the fall of Jerusalem plays a crucial role in dating these scriptures. Without question, AD 70 marks the climax of the Jewish War with the fall of the capital city. This comprised an event of such catastrophic proportions that *if* it had occurred before the writing of any of the epistles or gospels, they would have mentioned it. But they did not. We have no mentioning of it in any book. This provides us **an historical benchmark** for determining when those books arose. Since no author mentioned it anywhere, we stand on solid ground to take the entire New Testament canon as pre-dating AD 70. As Robinson said, AD 70 becomes the ceiling for the writing of the "New Testament." It also becomes a date that profoundly affects our interpretation of those writings.

CONCLUSION

The context of *where* someone says something makes a huge difference in terms of understanding. The words, "How are you?" takes on completely different meanings, connotations, and evaluations depending upon whether the speaker relates to you as a friend, a social acquaintance, a doctor, or a therapist! In the first case, the message becomes a communication of friendliness, in the next, of cultural politeness, in the third, of information gathering about one's health, and in the fourth, an invitation to disclose mental and emotional hurts. *Meaning entirely depends on the context.*

Likewise, *the context of where* the apocalyptic "end of the world" statements arose in the NT makes all the difference in the world for understanding and interpretation. The fact that they all occur *before* the looming shadow of the holocaust of Judaism, the fall of Jerusalem, and the end of theocratic Israel stand as highly significant. When a person ignores this NT context, that person invites all kinds of misunderstandings.

Chapter 4
**

INDEXING THE "WHAT"

The Story of "The End of the World"

What in the world transpired in AD 70 that made it one of the most important historical events in Judaism and Christianity? When I began to study eschatology, I truly did not think the events of AD 70 could have carried *that much importance*. I say that in spite of my theological training. Little did I know the critical importance of that date.

I soon discovered that AD 70 stood not only as *a* crucially important date, but perhaps **the** most crucially important date. After all, it marked the end of an era; it marked the end of a religion as it had existed (old covenant Judaism). Even today, many Orthodox Jews speak about AD 70 as "the end." With the holocaust that the Jewish-Roman War brought, Jerusalem fell and with it the Temple, the priesthood, the "Law" age of God's covenant with theocratic Israel. All these things came to a complete and abrupt end.

This date marked a crucial turning point for Christianity, a kind of second-beginning. It completed what began on Pentecost (Acts 2). It marked the transition between the old and new covenants.

Dr. Streeter (*The Four Gospels*) wrote,
> "It is impossible for us nowadays to realize *the shock of AD 70* to a community in which Jewish and Gentile members alike had been reared in the profoundest veneration of the immemorial sanctity of the Holy City and Temple" (p. 516).

Reading Streeter took me to the significant works of another scholar, S. G. F. Brandon.

Brandon wrote two scholarly works, *"The Fall of Jerusalem and The Christian Church,"* (1951) and *"Jesus and The Zealots"* (1967). In the first work he wrote,

> "Thus we may conclude that, after the Resurrection experiences, *the next most crucial event* in the life of the Christian Church was the overthrow of the Jewish nation, which was dramatically epitomized in the destruction of its holy city of Jerusalem in A.D. 70" (251).

These dates mark key facets of the "last days." In the last days, Jesus "was born under the law," incarnated in the flesh, manifested to Israel, suffered the cross, and resurrected from the dead. In those last days the apostles announced the beginning of the new covenant of grace that established the early Christian community. At the end of those last days a seven-year war with Rome occurred, the great tribulation, and the final fall of the theocracy. Via these events, the old world order of things came to an end that gave birth to the new world order of the new covenant.

All of this began with God's incarnation in human flesh which the Bible specifically says occurred "in these last days" (Heb. 1:1). God changed his *"modus operandi"* from speaking through the prophets to speaking through his son (Heb. 1:1-4). In those last days, the Logos took "flesh and dwelt among us" (John 1:1-14).

During those old covenant last days Jesus came, born of Mary "under the law" to redeem mankind from the curse of the law (Gal. 4:4-6). He became the Pascal lamb for both Israel and the world. Then at the cross, "all of our iniquities were put upon him" (Heb. 9:26, I Cor. 5:7, Isaiah 53, II Cor. 5:14-21). That initiated the new world of grace.

This redemptive act planted the word of the kingdom as *a seed* in the world. That seed first took root in the heart of those of the old theocracy. Eventually it began to expand beyond Israel to all nations. Finally, the harvest came. Then the old theocracy of fleshly Israel came to an end as the birthpangs of a new creation culminated in the full manifestation of "the sons of God" (Romans

8:17-29).   *What world ended?*   **The world of the Jewish theocratic state.** That world had its foundation in the Mosaic law, the priesthood of Aaron, and the old covenant (Heb. 7:18-19,22, 8:8-13). That world consisted of the old "heavens and earth" which God created for the old dispensation time and intended to soon replace with "the new heavens and new earth" of the new covenant time (Rev. 21-22).

"THE LATE GREAT JEWISH WORLD"
An Overview

If we run to the end of the end, then the final *coup de grace* of the Roman War against the Jewish commonwealth occurred on August, 22 AD 70. On that day of destruction the Zealots destroyed of one of the wonders of the ancient world--the Jewish Temple at Jerusalem. This occurred in August of 70 when the Romans broke through the fourth, and final wall, of Jerusalem and completely destroyed the holy city. They dismantled the Temple, tearing down "one stone upon another" as Jesus predicted (Matt. 24:1-4). What brought this about? What contributed to this destruction of a city and a religion?

To answer we have to back up to the year AD 66. In that year Emperor Nero ordered General Vespasian with the fifth and tenth Legions to crush the Jewish uprising which had gotten out of hand in Israel. The conflict centrally located between the radical Zealots and the Roman Empire. Yet between them stood Palestinian Christianity. Nor did that Hebraic Church play the role of an innocent bystander. Many within it became caught up with the Zealot movement and the nationalistic fervor that they became so nationalistically oriented that they even participated in the conflict.

Many identified with their Jewish brothers, the Zealots, against the Roman overlords. And no wonder. During this time *apocalyptism* grew into a mighty force. Everybody in that world had the feeling that the end would occur at any time!

During that same time the Messianic movement (the Christian Church) grew from infancy to adulthood and discovered its world-wide mission. By now the church began to lose many of its original apostles and pillars. The Jerusalem Church lost its great leader, James the Just when more fanatical Jews stoned him in AD 62. Shortly afterwards, in Rome, the Roman authorities killed Peter and Paul (AD 64-65). They suffered martyrdom when Nero blamed the burning of Rome on the Christians and set out to eliminate them.

Many Jewish Christians shared the concern of their brethren for their country and land. So many got caught up in *the apocalyptic fervor for freedom from Rome*. According to Josephus, the Zealot revolution spread "**a madness**" among the people. It was in the midst of these events that *I and II Peter* (AD 64), *Hebrews* (AD 64), and *Revelation* (AD 68) appeared as documents written to assist the early believers in coping with those apocalyptic times.

The Zealot rebellion instigated the war in 66 AD and ultimately the war came to an end when Rome wiped out the final resistance at the assault on Masada (AD 73). What provoked *this holocaust* that caused this little occupied country to become so completely destroyed? Why did the Romans so completely reject the Jews from their own land?

HOW THE MADNESS BEGAN

"The desolating sacrilege" in Israel began in AD 66 when the Zealot Jews revolted against Rome. Gessius Florus, the Roman governor, brought the rebellion to a head. Through those years, the Jewish population had constantly complained to Cestius Gallus, governor of Syria, against Gessius. But he scoffed at their outcry.

Then in AD 66, in the city of Caesarea some Greeks, who owned property next door to a synagogue, got into an antagonistic conflict with some of the young Jewish Zealots. This conflict escalated into insults, threats, and fist fights. To that, Gessius Florus over-responded. He brought in his soldiers who also over-reacted to the Jews. In the end, they killed and massacred 3,600 Jews, many of them peaceable citizens.

This totally enraged the fanatical hatred of the growing Zealot party. They reacted and used this totally unjust slaughter of their people to escalate the conflict into all out war. Even many Romans implored Florus to put a stop to the carnage (*The Jewish Wars,* Book Two, 443).

In reaction, the Zealots in July of that year (66) stormed Jerusalem and burned the palace of Agrippa and Bernice (Romans) and the palace of the Jewish High Priest Ananias (for his liberal affiliation with the Romans). They then massacred the whole Roman Garrison. This response not only escalated the hostilities, it began the revolt of the Jews against Rome.

Within five months, all of Palestine came into open rebellion against Rome. The fanatical Jews actually thought they could take on the world power(!). Josephus chronicles the war in his *"Wars of the Jews."* The story reads as one of escalation after escalation on the part of both until there was no way to stop the madness.

Immediately thereafter, the Syrians massacred 20,000 Jews at Caesarea. "The news of the disaster infuriated the whole nation, leading to reprisals from the Jews." From this beginning, the Roman-Jewish War ensued.

Josephus calls this war that horrible "epidemic of massacre" unparalleled in history. As the Romans massacred more and more Jews, they revenged themselves by laying waste with the sword and fire every city they could. At Damascus, the citizens shamefully butchered 10,500 unarmed and defenseless Jews. General Cestius marched the Roman Legions into Galilee.

Then a truly surprising event occurred. In a battle with the Jews, someone killed General Cestius. This represented an incredible turn of events! To the Romans it meant that the Jews (a little contemptible group of comparably untrained soldiers) had struck a stunning defeat against the invincible Roman Army!

When this news reached Emperor Nero, he became totally enraged (a response typical of his growing insanity). So he appointed Vespasian as General in charge of the Legions in Palestine and ordered him to completely crush Israel.

Concurrently, the Jewish leaders and Sanhedrin appointed *Josephus* as one of three Generals of the Jewish forces. He took leadership of the Galilean forces. Young Josephus (he had just turned 30 years of age) showed remarkable skills as a leader and thinker. Along with two other generals, the Jewish nation committed to him the leadership in organizing and implementing the Jewish response to Rome. At first, he focused his energies in fortifying many of the towns of Israel and fending off the Romans. He became highly successful in doing this.

Then things took a turn for the worse for Josephus. First, he unsuccessfully endeavored to attack Sepphoris. Later he wrote, "Galilee from end to end became a scene of fire and blood; from no misery, no calamity was it exempt; the one refuge for the hunted inhabitants was in the cities fortified by Josephus" (Book III, p. 595).

A short time afterwards (67 AD), Josephus met defeat at Jotapata. The Romans slew 40,000 of his soldiers and took another 12,200 of them as prisoners. General Josephus escaped with forty of his high ranking officers and hid in a cave. Then came about a series of events which completely changed the destiny of his life.

At that point, Josephus sent word to General Vespasian announcing that he wanted audience. Claiming himself as a prophet of God (after his biblical name sake, Joseph), Josephus said he had a very important message for Vespasian. Finding this intriguing, the Roman General sent to have the defeated General brought before him.

When Josephus appeared, he offered this prediction: Vespasian would one day become Emperor of Rome. "You are," Josephus said, "the man from the East" prophesied in the scriptures who would save Israel. This bemused Vespasian. And since he had his own hopes for the throne of Rome, Vespasian spared Josephus. Josephus proved so sincere and convincing that Vespasian appointed him as Recorder of War. [Josephus would travel with Vespasian (and later his son Titus), communicate to the refugee Jews behind the walls at Jerusalem, move to Rome to see the Parade of Victory, and wrote his books, *The Wars of the Jews*.]

As the war progressed in those years, and as the Romans decimated village after village, the refugees from every farm and town fled to the stronghold of Jerusalem. Titus, a Roman commander, went through the land conquering town after town. Consequently, in AD 67 and 68, Jerusalem swelled with the vast numbers of refugees as literally tens of thousands poured within her walls.

Yet the haven to which they fled (Jerusalem) became less and less a haven. Civil war raged there. The moderate Jews and the fanatical Zealots fought against each other. Josephus described John the Zealot leader and his 3,000 Idumean mercenary soldiers. They entered Jerusalem and "fell upon the people as a flock of profane animals, and cut their throats."

Then on June 9th, AD 68, the Roman Senate suddenly called General Vespasian from leading the war. Intense internal conflict in the city of Rome created havoc there for the Empire. Emperor Nero had made the Empire tremble with his madnesses. He had burned most of Rome to the ground so he could engage in a remodeling program; he persecuted the Christians furiously, and he began the War with Israel. Then suddenly in AD 68, he committed suicide. This ended his inglorious career as well as the house of Julius Caesar.

Yet before Vespasian got to Rome to claim the throne, a series of other generals took the title of Emperor of the Roman Empire. Yet one after another killed the preceding one. First Galba claimed to be Emperor, then Otho, then Vitellius. Things had become mighty unstable throughout the Empire.

Meanwhile, back in Jerusalem, the heat of the summer of AD 68 brought sickness and disease to the city. Simultaneously, in Rome a pestilence left tens of thousands dead. Other similar things occurred throughout the world. In Asia, city after city suffered from tremendous earthquakes. Eusebius, the historian, mentions Ephesus, Magnesia, Sardis, Aegae, Philadelphia, Tmolus, and Apollonia as sites of earthquakes. Seneca, the Roman historian, wrote, "The world itself is being shaken to pieces, and there is universal consternation" (Nat. Qu. VI.1). Such statements about that the chaos of that era certainly sound very much like the apocalyptic descriptions that Jesus told about

(Matthew 24).

By early spring of AD 69, the conditions within Jerusalem reached a critical mass. The barbarity of the Zealots grew worse and worse.

> "Every human ordinance was trampled under foot, every dictate of religion ridiculed by these men, who scoffed at the oracles of the prophets as impostors' fables. Yet those predictions of theirs contained much concerning virtue and vice, by the transgression of which the Zealots brought upon their country the fulfillment of the prophecies directed against it. For there was an ancient saying of inspired men that the city would be taken and the sanctuary burnt to the ground by right of war, whensoever it would be visited by sedition and native hands should be the first to defile God's sacred precincts" (Book IV, p.113).

Simon, son of Gioras, came to Jerusalem and brought it into even more dire distress.

> "With an insatiable lust for loot, [the Zealots] ransacked the houses of the wealthy; the murder of men and the violation of women were their sport; they caroused on their spoils, with blood to wash them down, and from mere satiety unscrupulously indulged in effeminate practices, plaiting their hair and attiring themselves in women's apparel, drenching themselves with perfumes and painting their eyelids to enhance their beauty..." (*Wars*, Book IV, p. 167).

As Vespasian left for Rome to claim the crown of Emperor, he encountered the soldiers of Roman Emperor Vitellius on the way. In the battle that ensued, Vespasian slew 50,000 Roman soldiers. Thereafter, the Congress in Rome proclaimed him the new Emperor of the Roman Empire. Yet before reaching Rome and securing the Imperial Crown, he had his young son, whose name happened to have been Domitian, assume the rule for a couple months, in his stead. Meanwhile, the Senate made his oldest son, Titus, General of the Legions in Palestine and commissioned him to finish the War against the Jews.

Finally came the year AD 70. Josephus' Book Five opens as a chronicle of that year. By then the besieged city of Jerusalem had become filled with death and devastation. Overcrowded and tormented with civil war between three factions lead by the priest

Eleazar, the Zealot John, and Revolutionary Simon, old Jerusalem had become a place of the dead. Corpses abounded. Those within the city began tossing hundreds of bodies over the walls daily.

Outside the city walls sat Titus with four legions just watching the death of the city. During this time, Titus ordered that his troops cut down every fruit tree (an event that disastrously effected the land for centuries up until our own century).

Sensing the end near, the Romans began to build up their earthworks and construct their battering rams. Shortly thereafter, the Legions broke through the first wall on May 25, AD 70, and the second wall a week later. By this time, hundreds of people deserted Jerusalem daily. At first, many of the nobles swallowed gold and silver coins before escaping, hoping to provide some wealth for themselves afterward. But when the Roman soldiers discovered this, they began a wholesale slaughter of those fleeing the city. They mercilessly struck down the deserters with their swords and "digged into their bowels for the gold and silver."

How did things far in the city? Deception and delusion prevailed.

> "Within the city the spirits of the war party, elated at their success, rose high; since they imagined that the Romans would never again venture into the city, or that, if they did, they themselves would prove invincible. For God was blinding their minds because of their transgressions" (Book V, 307, see I Thess. 2:14-16).

Also famine raged inside Jerusalem. It became so intense that some mothers actually boiled their babies which had died and ate their flesh. Josephus records the story of Mary, daughter of Eleazar, who did this to her son, August 16 (Book VI, p. 437).

As the year progressed, the Romans began capturing some 500 Jews escaping the city daily and crucified them. "The soldiers out of rage and hatred amused themselves by nailing their prisoners in different postures; and so great was their number, that space could not be found for the crosses nor crosses for the bodies" (341).

> "When Titus, going his rounds, beheld the valleys chocked with the dead [who had been thrown over the walls], and the thick matter oozing from under the clammy carcasses, he groaned and,

> raising his hands to heaven, called God to witness that this was not his doing" (361).

Josephus opened Book XI:
> "The sufferings of Jerusalem thus daily grew worse, the fury of the rebels being intensified by the calamities in which they were involved, and the famine now extending its ravages from the people to themselves. The piles of corpses throughout the city presenting a horrible spectacle and emitting a pestilential stench, were, moreover, an impediment to the combatants in their sallies; for, like men inured to countless carnage on the battlefield, they were compelled on the march to trample over the bodies" (Book VI, p. 379).

Then came the end of the old covenant sacrificial system. The daily sacrifice ceased in August of AD 70. About the same time the Romans broke through the third and fourth walls to make their final assault on the city. Then on **August 22, A.D. 70,** the Zealot Jews along with the Romans completely destroyed the Temple.

> "To narrate their enormities in detail is impossible," wrote Josephus, who witnessed the atrocities, "but, to put it briefly, no other city ever endured such miseries, nor since the world began has there been a generation more prolific in crime. ...It was they who overthrew the city, and compelled the reluctant Romans to register so melancholy a triumph, and all but attracted to the Temple the tardy flames. Verily, when from the upper town they beheld it burning, they neither grieved nor shed a tear, though in the Roman ranks these signs of emotion were detected" (Book V, p. 339).

Does that not sound like *"the great tribulation"* that Jesus predicted for his generation or not (Matthew 24:21, 34-35)? It speaks not only about the great tribulation that Israel suffered, it also speaks about *the end* of their old theocratic nation as they knew it.

Before the destruction of the Temple, Titus held a council with his staff concerning the Temple's fate.

> "Some were of opinion that the law of war should be enforced, since the Jews would never cease from rebellion while the Temple remained as the focus for concourse from every quarter. Others advised that if the Jews abandoned it and placed

no weapons whatever upon it, it should be saved, but that if they mounted it for purposes of warfare, it should be burnt; as it would then no longer be a temple, but a fortress, and thenceforward the impiety would be chargeable, not to the Romans but to those who forced them to take such measures."

"Titus, however, declared that, even were the Jews to mount it and fight therefrom, he would not wreck vengeance on inanimate objects instead of men, nor under any circumstances burn down so magnificent a work; for the loss would affect the Romans, inasmuch as it would be an ornament to the empire if it stood" (445).

As if things were not bad enough, *false prophets* arose to delude the people to the very end. One prophet urged all to go to the Temple saying that they could expect God to come and rescue them there. They went. And as they did, the invading Romans soldiers forthrightly slew them. Josephus also tells about signs that appeared in those days. He told about a "star resembling a sword that stood over the city."

Josephus wrote about some strange oracles that floated about the populace within the city. These very well could have been the original scroll of what we now call *the book of Revelation*. He says that within these oracles, someone recorded a message "that the city and the sanctuary would be taken away when the temple should become four-square." That sounds like Revelation's city four-square--a description of the new covenant (See Chapter 10).

Josephus as one who did not believe in Jesus, explained the oracle in this way:

"What more than all else incited them to the war was *an ambiguous oracle*, likewise found in their sacred scriptures, to the effect that at that time one from their country would become ruler of the world [Jesus!?]. This they understood to mean someone of their own race, and many of their wise men went astray in their interpretation of it. The oracle, however, in reality signified the sovereignty of Vespasian, who was proclaimed Emperor on Jewish soil" (467).

Then came the end of the Temple. "You would have indeed thought that the Temple-hill was boiling over from its base," wrote Josephus, "being everywhere one mass of flame, but yet that the stream of blood was more copious than the flames and the slain more numerous than the slayers. For the ground was nowhere visible through the corpses; but the soldiers had to clamber over heaps of bodies in pursuit of the fugitives" (457).

Afterward, the Romans razed the Temple to the ground as the Romans went after the melted gold that flowed down between the huge stones.

After the one million, one hundred thousand who perished in the fall of Jerusalem, the Romans took 97,000 of the young men and women as slaves. They took them to the theaters in the region, and then on to Rome.

THE DAY AFTER
Events After The World Ended

Josephus' Book VII begins with a description of Jerusalem several months later its destruction. These words, from the biblical covenant theology standpoint, refer to the time after the old covenant world ended.

> "All the rest of the wall encompassing the city was so completely leveled to the ground as to leave future visitors to the spot no ground for believing that it had ever been inhabited. Such was the end to which the frenzy of revolutionaries brought Jerusalem, that splendid city of world-wide renown" (*Wars*, Book VII, p. 505).

After the destruction, General Titus went to Caesarea to rest. While resting he brought out 2,500 of his prisoners from Jerusalem. There, in October, he had them fight with wild beasts in the Coliseum for entertainment(!). Afterwards, he revisited Jerusalem. He took all the treasures that he had gathered, along with 100,000 slaves, and went back to Rome for a triumphal procession.

Today, nearly two-thousand years later, the Arch of Titus still stands in Rome as a memorial of that procession. In AD 72-73, the rest of the Legions brought an end to Zealots' resistance at Masada. About that same time, the Romans demolished the Jewish Temple of Onias in Egypt (near Alexandria). Here lived the second largest Jewish community in that ancient world (AD 73).

Later (AD 75), the Romans erected a Roman Temple (named Templum Pacis) on the site where Solomon's original Temple had stood.

AN EPIC CATASTROPHE
OF BIBLICAL PROPORTIONS!

If you want to accurately index the references in the text of the NT with regard to eschatology and "the end of the world," you need to understand this socio-political environment within which those documents arose. For out of that social, political, and religious setting the apocalyptic literature of the NT came into existence. Out of this background the Jewish-Roman War occurred which, in turn, brought an end to Old Testament Israel.

Those turbulent and traumatizing times came upon the believers just as the forty-year transition period came to an end. At the end, the seven-years war had reduced Palestine to rubble. The destruction of Jerusalem became a trauma of enormous proportions to Jewish consciousness and with it old covenant Judaism came to an end. Thirty years later, unknown authors wrote "the Apocalypse of Ezra" and the "Syriac Apocalypse of Baruch" to deal with that physical and spiritual trauma.

To note the psychological effect of that trauma, we might draw a similar comparison with the catastrophe of the Second World War in our time. The Nazis' holocaust involved the torture and destruction of millions of people now dates some 50 years ago. Yet it still evokes highly intense emotions for those who lived through that period as well as for those who observed their torment.

A few years back (1987), then President Ronald Reagan planned a ten-minute visit to a German graveyard. Do you remember what then happened? In response to that announcement, people became violent. They protested vigorously. They said it would validate the Nazi government! Obviously, that trauma continued to function as if very much alive, and explosive, within their minds and hearts fifty years later!

This makes Dr. Streeter's (*The Four Gospels*) words especially poignant regarding the events of AD 70.

> "It is impossible for us nowadays to realize the shock of AD 70 to a community in which Jewish and Gentile members alike had been reared in the profoundest veneration of the immemorial sanctity of the Holy City and Temple" (p. 516).

This Jewish catastrophe meant the end of the Jewish nation as God's theocratic nation. It consisted of an "epic event of biblical proportions."

> "The Jews did, then, indeed receive a blow from which, as a nation, they never recovered. Although later, in the time of Hadrian, they rose once more in armed revolt against Rome, their national existence had really terminated in AD 70, for on the razed site of their Holy City a heathen soldiery now had its camp" (Brandon, 1951, p. 166).
>
> "Thus we may conclude that, after the Resurrection experiences, the next most crucial event in the life of the Christian Church was the overthrow of the Jewish nation, which was dramatically epitomized in the destruction of its holy city of Jerusalem in A.D. 70" (251).

The destruction of the Temple represented a major crisis for Judaism because of all the Temple symbolized for them. It meant "the Presence of God" (the Shekinah of glory), the place of the daily sacrifice (the cultus), Israel's place in election, etc. had shifted its place. Negatively, AD 70 brought an end to all of that. It brought the final judgment so often spoken about in the parables and apocalyptic statements of Jesus.

Positively, these events meant *the establishment and completion of the new covenant*. It meant "the perfect" (the completion) had come (I Cor. 13:8-13). It meant that now the Shekinah of glory shifted to a completely internal reality (in the hearts of men), the priestly sacrifice of Christ totally replaced the old, and God now reckons all persons of faith as elected in Christ and as the new Israel of God (Gal. 6:16, Rom. 2:28-29).

Two groups experienced this fall of Jerusalem and the end of the theocracy world as especially traumatic: the Jewish race and the believers in Christ "zealous for the law." No wonder then that so much in the NT speaks about these (then) upcoming events. It radically affected the source of salvation. After all, "salvation is from the Jews" (John 4:22). Yet the conservative (fundamentalist) Jerusalem Church slowly resisted the transition into the new age of Christ's new covenant.

The conservative Palestinian Hebrew branch of Christianity even included the "sect of the Pharisees which believed." And before the end they dominated the mother church. No wonder they viewed Paul's liberal ministry with a jaundiced eye (Acts 15:5). As thoroughly Jewish, they continued to observe the old ways (Acts 15:1). As late as AD 59 their leader James urged Paul to take a vow in the Temple because tens of thousands of Jews who believed "and they are all zealous of the law" (Acts 21:20-21).

Palestinian Christianity consisted of an entirely Jewish orientation in background, heritage, practice, and hope. This explains the problem that the author of *Hebrews* addressed no longer exists. It no longer exists as a possibility today. What problem did *Hebrews* refer to? The problem of giving up faith in Jesus as the Messiah and returning to the old covenant as manifested in theocratic Israel with their Temple, worship, sacrifice, priests, etc. An unknown author wrote *Hebrews* against the backdrop of the Jewish-Roman War. No wonder the writer urged the Palestinian believers to "go forth unto (Jesus) outside the camp, bearing abuse for him" (Heb. 13:13). (See Chapter 6).

Concurrent to that trauma occurred another one caused by *the monster Nero* during the sixties. At that time Nero's incipient insanity erupted. He set the fire in Rome which burned for ten days and leveled ten of its fourteen districts. To divert blame, he accused the Christians of incendiarism (the crime of setting the fire). That began the most deliberately sadistic persecutions. Nero had Christians sown up in the skins of wild animals upon whom he set loose savage hunting dogs. He had them enclosed in sacks with stones and flung into the Tiber River. He had them coated with pitch and set alight to light his palace gardens. Both apostles Peter and Paul suffered martyrdom in 64 and 65 AD at the hands of that monster on Rome's throne.

When these traumatic events began to take place, many of the early Christians wondered if *the Messianic Age* had indeed begun. Wouldn't you? They began questioning whether Jesus indeed had become Lord. Did his apostles tell the truth? Did their faith in the new covenant have a solid foundation to stand on? Would things get better?

The Palestinian Christians felt powerless against Imperial Rome. They felt inferior in the eyes of their Jewish brethren who treated them as apostates. Daily hostility grew within orthodox Judaism against them. Jewish non-believers chased and persecuted Paul from town to town (Acts chs. 13-21). And with all this pressure and persecution, many of them began to regress to childish reactions. Subsequently, the NT writers addressed this regression (Heb. 5:11-14, 6:6-20, 12:1-15, I Corinthians).

SO WHAT HAPPENED?
Did the Church Leave Babylon and "Come Out?"

The Jewish-Christians and most of Palestinian Christianity *probably perished in the Fall of Jerusalem*. Some did escape to Pella, others to Alexandria, and others to Asia Minor--they became "raptured" out of the great tribulation. But many, if not most, undoubtedly failed to take the words of Jesus seriously. They held on to their nationalistic hopes believing that Jesus would save them from their nation's judgment.

In the fourth century, church historian Eusebius preserved an ancient quote. It alleged that the Jerusalem Church fled into the wilderness prior to the fall of Jerusalem. Eusebius stands as our oldest authority for the Pella Flight.

> "When the people of the church in Jerusalem, having been commanded by an oracle, given by revelation to men approved before the war, to depart from the city and to dwell in a certain city of Peraea, namely, Pella, (and) when those who believed on Christ had migrated thither from Jerusalem, so that the royal city of the Jews and the whole land of Judea had been utterly forsaken by holy men, the judgment of God finally overtook those who had abused Christ and his apostles and completely wiped out that generation from among men." (Ecclesiastica

Historica, III. v.2-3, vi.4).

Eusebius quoted Epiphanius, a second century Christian writer, as his source. Did the Jerusalem Church escape? Did they get "raptured" out of the doomed city before the Judgment of God fell?

Professor Brandon, and others, doubt that the entire Jerusalem Church made the Pella flight. Lloyd Gaston (1970) wrote: "Most of the Jerusalem Church did not survive the War of 66-70" (p. 142). Why? For one thing, after that flight, the "Jerusalem" Church produced no extant literature. And if the influential mother Church produced no literature in Pella, they must not have fled there. Yet historical evidence offers scanty indications compared to the records we have of other first and second century churches.

Brandon sees in Matthew 10:5-6 a possible suggestion that members of the Jerusalem Church scattered throughout the cities of Palestine. I question this. For could not the mother church flee to Pella and *not* produce literature? I think so.

The trauma of the flight, of the war, of the shock to their way of life, all could have resulted in them producing in little to no literature. Further, some of the refugees could have fled to Alexandria in Egypt. After all, Alexandria became a flourishing center of Christian life in the second century. And, I would also guess that many of them simply did not heed Christ's warning and so suffered that judgment day along with their countrymen. They, to whom the word came, simply did not "give heed" to the voice that spoke to them from heaven (Heb. 12:25-29, 2:1-3). This would make meaningful *Revelation* and *Hebrews* that targeted them and tried to get them to change their thinking and "come out from among them" (Rev. 18:4). When they did not, they ended up suffering the judgment of their countrymen.

Rupert Furneaux (1972) wrote:
> "It seems probable that the Christians remained in Jerusalem sharing their countrymen's glorious cause. Like their friends the Zealots, they were buoyed up by hopes of divine deliverance" (146).

S. G. F. Brandon (1951) said that in view of the former unique authority and prestige of the Jerusalem Church

> "the conclusion appears in every way reasonable and necessary that the Jerusalem Church fell together with the Jewish nation in the catastrophe of AD 70 because that Church in its principles and the loyalties of its members was essentially one with the nation" (180).

Brandon (1967) argued for an almost total annihilation of the Jerusalem Church.

> "If this church had indeed migrated elsewhere before the roman siege, it would surely have continued to enjoy its prestige among Christians; as did, for example, among the Jews, the rabbinical school founded by rabbi Johanan ben Zakkai at Jamnia after his flight from the doomed metropolis" (p. 15).

Yet we must remember that prior to 1949, we knew little to nothing about the Qumran community in the Dead Sea wilderness. The volumes of Dead Sea Scrolls that now inform us about that community laid hidden in the clay jars in AD 68 as they saw the coming judgment. But the Jerusalem Church may have not hidden their books and scrolls if they really didn't expect their Nation destroyed.

I see another difference. The Jews escaped and established a reformed Judaism based on the Torah instead of the Temple. That established their prestige. But the Jewish Palestinian-Christians who escaped lost their prestige inasmuch as their former prestige existed *because* they were all "zealous for the law" (Acts 21:21).

In America today, we have various "Christian militarist" groups who have made American nationalism a part of their creed. A similar phenomenon occurred in the first century when some Jewish Christians made Jewish nationalism a part of the "gospel." By making too much out of Jewish nationalism (Zionism) they subverted the gospel.

Robert A. Aytoun (1915) tells us that in the post-Jerusalem history, a small Pella community returned to Jerusalem in AD 136 (City Centres Of Early Christianity). Gibbon noted the same event, that the Jerusalem Church returned, and added that they returned with Marcus as bishop--a Gentile. That surely served as the ultimate sign of the purging of Judaism from the mother church. Further, Dr. Rendel Harris believes that the *Odes of*

Solomon, an early Christian hymn book, possibly resulted from that Church at Pella.

This realization of what happened to the Jerusalem Church strikes me as truly sad and pathetic. Especially given all of the scriptures which are full of instruction and warnings to the early believers about coming out of Jewish legalism. Yet when it came down to it, great numbers of the early Hebrew Palestinian Christians apparently did not, or could not, make the break. They went down with their countrymen. Did some stay to preach and warn them? Did some get caught up in the Zealot movement? We do not know. What do we know? Only that the Church in Jerusalem never again became a major center of the Christian faith.

This sober history gives new meaning to Peter's warning, "For the time has come for *judgment to begin with the household of God;* and if it begins with us, what will be the end of those who do not obey the gospel of God?" (I Pet. 4:17). It also gives new meaning to those passages in *Hebrews*, *I Peter*, and *Revelation* that warn the Christians about Judaizing the Gospel. For me it explains the nature of the conflict, one between the Jews and the "true Israel" in *Revelation* (2:9, 3:9-12, 11:8).

CONCLUSION

When the biblical writers talk about "the end" and all of the eschatological events of the end, they directed all of their talk exclusively to *the end of the Jewish theocratic nation and of the covenant of law*. None of the end-of-the-world language, predictions, or warnings within the pages of the NT concerned the end of the Christian age, the Kingdom, or the planet earth. The new era of the covenant of grace would last forever, "world without end."

INDEXING
When, Where, Who, What, How, and Why Regarding *The End of the World*

The Cross and the Parousia

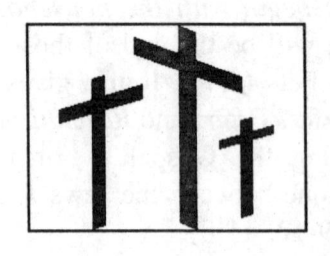

"*The New Israel Of God*"

"The last days... of the Old Covenant of Theocratic Israel"

What?
End of the Old
Beginning of the
New world/covenant

When?
Soon, shortly,
"at hand" in
this generation

Where?
In Roman
occupied
Israel, 1st.c.

Who?
Theocratic
Israel
"Salvation
is of the Jews"

Clouds of Heaven
Clouds of Judgment/Victory

"The New Heavens
& New Earth"

✳

A.D. 70   Covenant Promises

How?
Judgment on fleshly Israel separates believing from unbelieving

Language?
Hebraic Apocalypism about an age-changing Event

Why?
To complete covenant blessings to Abraham to All Nations; to complete the new covenant gospel of grace; to separate Christianity as a sect of Judaism and free it to become an Ecumenical fellowship of believers

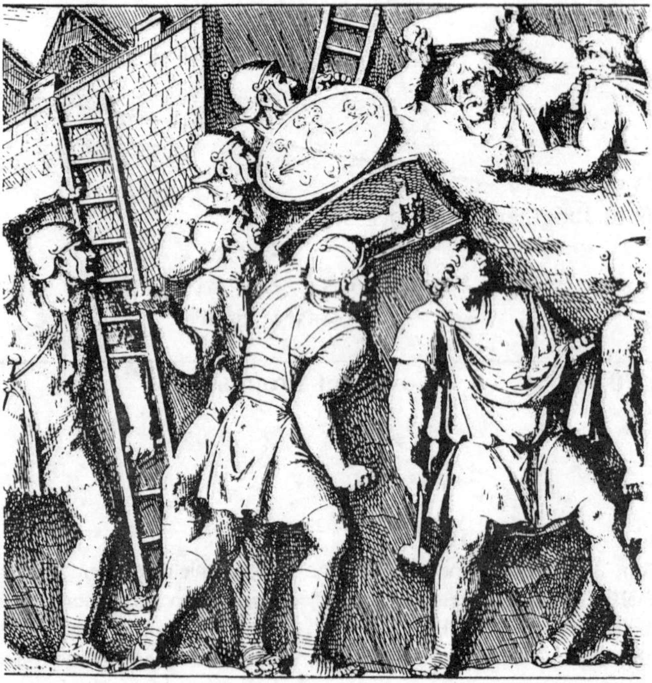

Chapter 5
**

INDEXING THE WHO

*"To Who and About Whom does 'the End' Apply?
"Who did Jesus, et al. target
regarding the 'at hand' End?"*

If you tune into radio and television broadcasts today you will come away with the impression that all of the Bible's statements that the end of the world **exists right now** *"at hand"* and that the apostles wrote those statements direction *to you*. Amazing don't you think? It just so happens that **you** live in the very generation that Jesus spoke to about "the end!" You live in the last generation!

But *if* you begin with the biblical context itself, you will undoubtedly receive an entirely different impression. I think, in fact, that you would have no problem at all *indexing the who*. You would come away with the impression that **Jesus addressed his generation**. These people comprise the audience of his speeches. More specifically, you would realize that he spoke to that generation of Jews before him and that he spoke about the end of **that world** --the old covenant world of law (Judaism).

This fits biblical theology. After all, "salvation is from the Jews" (John 4:22). By that statement, Jesus meant salvation would come through the Jewish nation and through the Jewish Messiah. Accordingly, after the *initial* changing of the covenants (on Pentecost, Acts 2), the Jews first received word of the good-news of grace. They comprise the first ones in the new order of things.

Paul said the gospel went out "to the Jews first" (Romans 1:16-17). Then it evolved. Then it began to go out to other nations (Acts 8-10). Later, it went out "to the Gentile."

When that happened the new covenant community's "Jewish problem" began. Even many of the believing Jews did not like it. The more fundamentalistic and Zionistic among them began persecuting Paul over his apostleship to the Gentiles (Acts 13-28). Eventually, when enough Gentiles had accepted the gospel of grace, the Jewish problem arose with a new intensity, "What about the Jews?" "What role did or do they play in the changing of the covenants?"

PAUL'S DOCUMENT ON "THE JEWISH PROBLEM"
Romans 9-11

Paul addressed the question of the Jews when he wrote *Romans*. He there devoted *three chapters in his "Romans" treatise* to this problem. Within this work he documented God's plan of good-news ("gospel") for setting things right between man and God by means of the new covenant of grace (1:16-17). By this grace covenant people become enabled to live by the spirit, rather than by the letter of the law (Rom. 7:6).

In Romans, Paul devoted the first three chapters to establishing the need for the good-news. He described man's godlessness, crimes, and general disempowerment (Ch. 1-3). Then he detailed the content of the good-news; God's salvation acts through the person of Jesus (3:21-31). Next came the process by which one appropriates that grace via the Abrahamic faith-process (Ch. 4). He then provided a wonderful list of the rich resources that faith-righteousness initiates (the list of empowering resources that make people full and complete (5:1-11).

Then, Paul described how the gospel facilitates a transformation in our state from being in the dimension of old adam (old man) to the new (5:12-21, 6:1-11). This grace generates an entirely new mental focus (6:12-23) for living in the new world with newness of life. He utilized the metaphor of a new marriage relationship to describe this experience of intimacy with God. This new relational reality empowers people to live in newness of spirit rather than oldness of flesh (7:1-6). That arises because it declares that God totally accepts believers as beloved children and winners (7:7- 8:39).

What else did Paul need to say about *this wild and wonderful covenant of grace* that rescues people from law-righteousness? Two things.

First, the Jewish questions. If all this came "from" the Jews (the old covenant that promised blessings to all people through Abraham) then what does this imply about that old covenant of law and about the theocratic nation of Israel? After all, Israel served as the source and origin of the gospel. So if grace-righteousness (received by faith) serves as the new way in this new era, and we exist "no longer under law, but under grace" (6:14-15), then *what about Israel according to the flesh?*

Second, the life-style question. If this whole new world of spirit has come, *how shall we live out the transformed life in our everyday walk?* Paul addressed the Jewish question in three chapters (Romans 9-11). Then he addressed the life-style question in five chapters (Romans 12-16). Since the first speaks to the issue of theocratic Israel's place in covenant history, before and after the consummation in Christ's new covenant, it enables us to understand and **index the who** regarding the "last things."

THEOCRATIC ISRAEL'S PLACE IN COVENANT HISTORY

The text of Romans 9-11 addresses the place, status, and meaning of covenant Israel in God's gospel plan. Reading it will usher you into a literary section loaded with OT scriptures and Hebraic thinking. It demonstrates rabbinical thought patterns and Hebraic literary expressions, and yet for all that you will find its message very gospel. So why the reasoning patterns characterized by the way the rabbis reasoned with language expressions unique to the rabbis of that period? Paul's design comprised relating OT theology to new covenant fulfillment. No wonder most people find this literary piece as simultaneously difficult fascinating. This undoubtedly explains why so much misunderstanding has resulted from this section.

As we begin to analyze and interpret these verses, *pay special attention to Paul's use of questions*. He baptizes the section in questions! First, Paul discloses his own personal feelings about this issue (9:1-5). Then he structures these 90 verses around questions and answers. This suggests to me that he probably wrote this section to summarize the questions (and kind of questions) that people had posed to him. Today his answers provide us with an understanding of *covenant theology* in terms of how God's covenant (to the fathers) moved through Israel to all nations.

1. Has the word of God failed? (9:6-13).
2. Does God show unjustness? (9:14-18).
3. Why does God find fault? (9:19-29).
4. How have the Gentiles found faith-righteousness while Israel has not? (9:30-10:4).
5. What does faith-righteousness say? (10:5-17).
6. How has Israel not heard the word? (10:18-21).
7. Has God rejected his people? (11:1-6).
8. What conclusion about Israel can we draw? (11:7-10).
9. Did they fall irrevocably? (11:11-32).
10. Doxology to God's unfathomable love (11:33-36).

In 90 verses Paul presented a theology of covenant and theodicy. *Covenant* focused on God's "promised word" to Abraham and how that promised word worked out in the history of the theocracy (Israel) regarding God's ultimate design of creating sons and daughters. These he called to become "conformed to the image of his Son" (8:28-29). Paul presented an understanding of God's criteria for determining who he accepts and who he rejects. As you read it, notice all of *the covenant theology words* (promise, word, call, election, faith/works, rejection, justice, fault, glory, mercy, remnant, etc.).

Theodicy focused on why "bad things" happen and continue to happen to Israel according to the flesh. Namely, their so-called "rejection" from Christ. Theodicy also focused on how we can recognize God as just while rejecting those whom he had called (the nation of Israel). Answer: they refused to trust in his Messiah. The good-news? If they will now believe, God will save them. All Israel, in fact, shall become saved by faith in the Messiah.

COVENANT INTEGRITY

Suppose you wanted to follow the progression of God's promised covenant word to Abraham through the Bible. Where would you begin? Why not start, as Paul did, with the word of promise containing "the Abrahamic Promise and Covenant" (Gen. 12:1-3)? "The scripture, foreseeing that God would justify the Gentiles by faith, preached the gospel beforehand to Abraham, saying, 'In thy seed shall all nations be blessed'" (Gal. 3:8).

What did God want to do with Abraham? He sought to bring *a people* into the world, to locate them in *a special land*, so that *a special descendent* within that lineage would one day become "the seed" who would create "the blessing" for all nations. The Abrahamic Covenant promise involved three facets: the *theocratic* nation of Israel (not just the nation of Israel), the land of Canaan given by Joshua, and the Messiah (Christ).

The theocratic nation experienced an experiment in law divinely designed to "bring them to Christ" (Gal. 3:6-28). As the specially chosen people, God called upon them to become "the light to the nations." The special land, which just happened to lie in the middle of all of the trade-routes of the ancient world(!), indicated their divine designation not to segregate Israel away from the Gentiles, but to become the center. Jerusalem would become the place where all nations would flow.

In this way, *people and land* functioned in a way secondarily to *the seed*. People and land served God's vessels for bringing **the light** into the world (John 1:1-5) and for preparing the world for receiving the messiah. Then the messiah would create a blessing of grace (forgiveness, love, reconciliation, renewal, spirit, resourcefulness, etc.) that would bless all nations (John 1:14-18).

But national Israel got these things mixed up. Rather than catching the vision of functioning as God's light of the world to others, they thought of themselves as God's light unto themselves. So they turned inward. In the end, they focused attention on the people and land to the exclusion of the seed. This sabotaged their long-term mission (providing the context for the seed) to the short-term and means-values of land and people. When the promised "word of God" to Abraham became *fulfilled in the early Christian church*, that word did *not* fail just because many in the nation of Israel did not come in (Rom. 9:6).

Why not? Because of **the principle** "not all who are descended from Israel, belong to Israel" (9:7). Merely descending from Abraham physically had never guaranteed belonging. *Belonging* had never depended on the flesh. It had always depended on the promise (9:8). God issues calls of grace and mercy because the essence of his glory and presence comprises mercy (9:14).

The experience of rejection never occurs because God throws the dice and thereby picks some and rejects others. The biblical picture of pre-destining involves God choosing to *grace* people. Those who accept, receive, and utilize become *the chosen*, and those who reject, deny, and refuse to use become *the rejected* (9:14-29). He predestines us to experience grace--how we respond depends on our faith.

This describes the truth about God's dealings with Pharaoh. God raised him up to "make known his power" (9:22), yet Pharaoh hardened his heart again and again every time God graciously released the plagues at Pharaoh's request. Pharaoh had an ego problem. It galled him that Someone had more ultimate power than himself. He hated that! So when God demonstrated His power to Pharaoh, the Egyptian monarch "hardened his heart" *against God's mercies* (not God's harshness). His pride, arrogance, and rigidness prevented him from recognizing the presence and majesty of God and glorying in it.

Yes, God seeks to mold man as a potter molds clay (9:19-29). Yet there exists a difference. What difference should we recognize? Namely, that the kind of clay a potter has to deal with in man concerns his God-given ability to "answer back to God." Man can resist God's purposes! God has put that much power into human hands. Simultaneously, we cannot play God, assuming that our destinies lies entirely in our hands. The design and purpose of our existence does not in our hands. The potter has the right to establish his plans and to carry out his covenant promises and to bring in the Gentiles (9:24ff).

The grand conclusion? ("What shall we say, then?")

> "That Gentiles who did not pursue righteousness have attained it, that is, righteousness through faith; but that Israel who pursued the righteousness based on law did not succeed in fulfilling that law..." (9:30-33).

What describes the heart of Paul's meaning in Romans 9? How should one determine its meaning? Two *hermeneutical principles* to guide us. (1) Always go first to the clear and obvious language, the propositional "straight" language of the text (if there you can find any). (2) Then, use the author's own conclusions to understand his arguments (i.e. line of reasoning).

Let's apply this. (1) First, notice the clear and obvious language of Romans 9. "What shall we say then? The Gentiles who did not pursue righteousness have attained it, i.e. righteousness through faith; but that Israel who pursued the righteousness which is based on law did not succeed in fulfilling that law. Why? Because they did not pursue it through faith, but as it were based on works" (9:30-32).

We cannot get clearer, plainer, "straighter," or more propositional than that. Any misunderstanding about that? One got it; one did not. Those outside covenant relationship (the Gentiles) attained faith-righteousness; those within covenant relationship failed, did not succeed. Why? Because of their law-orientation.

Read the passage again. Does it not really underscore *personal responsibility*? Yes it does! The gospel holds all people responsible for receiving God's righteousness "by faith" rather than by law (Rom. 1:16-17). It becomes available by faith, not by law (10:1-4). Try to establish your own righteousness based on works, on deeds, on self-righteousness and it will not work. "For no human being will be justified in His sight by works of law" (3:20). The gospel holds all people responsible before God to receive the righteousness of Christ. Does not Paul make that conclusion clear?

In this way *the conclusion must control the argument*. Given this conclusion in Romans 9, it therefore must consist of *the meaning* of Paul's line of reasoning and must control our interpretation of his reasoning. In other words, if we use Romans 9 and Paul's arguments and come up with anything contrary to his conclusion, then **we** must misunderstand his point.

I belabor all this to emphasize that whatever ideas or beliefs you have regarding "predestination," about God hardening the heart of whomsoever he wills, about rejecting theocratic Israel, about selecting the remnant, etc., that if it goes against and contradicts *the personal responsibility* of all people as indicated in his summary (9:30-33), then you have misunderstood that text.

Paul's line of reasoning in Romans 9-10 says that God's covenant word of promise to Abraham has always functioned as a word given to the "faith"-ful in response to the promise, not based on something external like genealogy (9:6-13). Paul argues that God only and always predestines *mercy*, but **how** a person responds to mercy depends on his own human clay--whether he will or will not yield to God's molding (9:14-29). There always exists *"if"-ness* in God's predestined words (Jer. 18:1-12, quoted in Rom. 9:20). God only predestines *the process*, not the persons. Whether someone chooses to become chosen (elects to become elected) rests as their free-choice.

This theme, in fact, continues throughout Chapter 10. Theocratic Israel, for the most part, has opted out of the program because their legalism blinded them (10:1-4). Yet to *opt back in* consists of one simple step. Opting back in requires no transcendent spiritual experience (ascending to heaven), nor mourner's bench wretchedness (descending into the abyss). It only requires acknowledging and confessing reality--**Jesus as Lord** (10:5-13). The apostolic church has declared this message of the Jesus Salvific Events (resurrected to lordship) to the whole world

(10:14-21).

What then consists of the problem? *Stubbornness.* Foolish stubbornness! They wanted to establish their own righteousness rather than submit to the righteousness of God. This foolish stubbornness blinded them to the offer of good-news.

THE SALVATION OF THE JEWS
It Means What It Means, Not What It Says!

"How do you understand *the salvation of the Jews* according to Romans 11?" First, Israel can definitely experience salvation! What proof do you have for that? Paul himself has experienced salvation and he exists as "an Israelite, a descendant of Abraham, a member of the tribe of Benjamin." So too can any Israelite (11:1).

The rejection of unbelieving Israel follows the pattern God used in dealing with Israel during Elijah's time (11:2-6), in Isaiah's time (11:7-8/ Isa. 29), and during David's time (11:9-10/ Psalm 69). What pattern do those scriptures reference? That *God saves by grace, not works* (11:6), and that "hardness" functions from human choice.

Has Israel irrevocably fallen in their rejection? No! (11:11). God uses his grace to the Gentiles to provoke jealousy in Israel (11:11-24), hoping that they won't want to stay out, but will want to get in on the blessings.

The Olive Tree of the Abrahamic covenant has roots in God's promises. It first gave birth to the branches of theocratic Israel. However, since connection to those roots occurs "by faith" (11:20), as the Gentiles can become grafted in, so can Israel. It occurs entirely as a matter of individual faith, not racial heritage. Each can also become rejected by prideful unbelief (11:20).

This reflects a major change and difference between the old and new covenants. Old covenant functioned as a national and racial process. A person entered it due to his/her race. The new covenant functions as a personal and faith-driven process. A person enters and experiences it according to acceptance of grace.

In this way all Israel can become saved. "And so all Israel will be saved..." (11:26). The *"so"* here functions as an adverb--an adverb of manner. This means it refers to *the way in which* Israel will experience salvation. Several translations read, "And *in this manner* all Israel will be saved."

What manner? The manner in which the gospel says anyone can becomes saved --*"by faith,"* i.e. by faith in the messiah. Hence the words, "as it is written, 'The Deliverer will come from Zion, he will banish ungodliness from Jacob'; 'and this will be my covenant with them when I take away their sins'" (11:26-7).

What manner will salvation occur for Israel? By believing in the Zion Deliverer (Jesus) who establishes the new covenant of forgiveness (Jer. 31:31-34). There exists no other way! "All Israel" will not and cannot become saved *en masse* apart from the faith of individual persons. They will become saved "in this manner." All Israel shall become saved in that manner; that represents God's hope, desire, gift, and call.

Yes, right now from *the AD 59 perspective of the book's date* Israel served as a big pain in the side of the church. Zealots chased, persecuted, and tortured Paul everywhere he went. They made his life a living hell (I Thess. 2:14-16). Hence, "as regards the gospel, they are enemies of God" (11:28).

Yet, "as regards election they are beloved for the sake of their forefathers, for the gifts and the call of God are irrevocable" (11:29). God still loves the Jews! Nor does He have any intention of changing his gift (eternal life) or his call to them (invitation of the gospel). God invites and welcomes them in spite of their antagonistic behaviors.

Why so much patience and kindness and love on God's part? Because "mercy" expresses God's ultimate character! More than anything else, he wants to show mercy (11:31-32). This depth of love stands as the mystery of his wisdom and knowledge so unsearchable and inscrutable (11:33). It does not describe the way we work nor our way of responding to enemies. But it expresses God's!

God's way of saving all Israel involves the same way that he offers to all. "For, 'Every one who calls upon the name of the

Lord will be saved.'" (10:13). "For there is no distinction between Jew and Greek; the same Lord is Lord of all and bestows his riches upon all who call upon him." (10:12). This locates the meaning of "and so all Israel will be saved." In English, it does *not* mean what it sounds like. Its meaning arises from what its author meant *in context*. We have to let the gospel interpret these words. We have to index it to the entire section (Rom. 9-11) and to the entire epistle.

CONCLUSION

Since the phrase, "the last days," in the biblical text refers to *the last days of Israel* (Heb. 1:1ff), we need to remember that the authors made statements about the nearness of the end to fleshly theocratic Israel. God had not created and called the theocratic nation into existence as an end in itself. He created his son Israel as a means to an end, namely, to bring in the Messiah through whom God could "bless all nations." The role of the nation of Israel served its purpose and came to an end.

Thus the people of Israel, like the people of all other nations and races, could then come into the new world of grace, spirit, forgiveness, love, and power. Sadly, many refused. They erroneously wanted special privilege. They viewed equality with the Gentiles as an insult. But the good-news of the new covenant stands that "in Christ Jesus there is neither male nor female" (sexual gender distinctions), "bond nor free" (social distinctions), "Jew nor Greek" (racial distinctions) (Gal. 3:27-29).

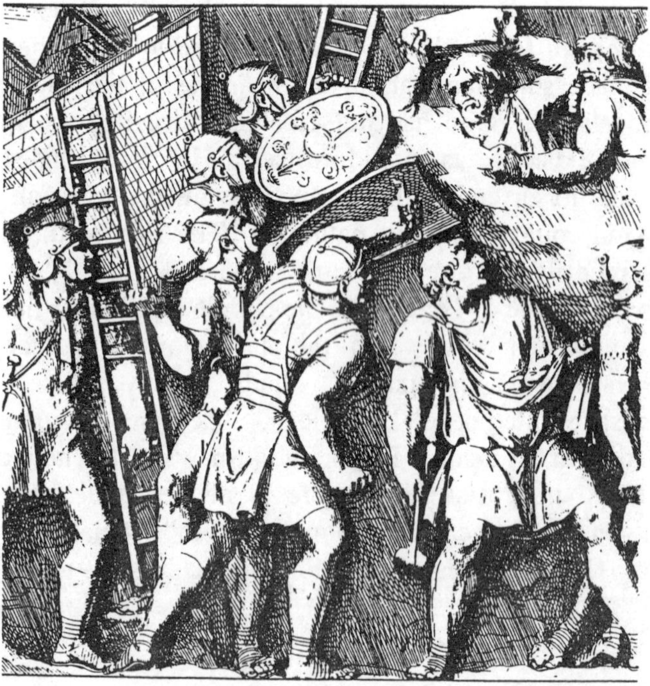

Chapter 6
**

INDEXING WHO ACCORDING TO THE BOOK OF "HEBREWS"

The Jewish Believers at the Mother Church

Did anyone other than Paul and his treatise to the Romans address what we have called *"the Jewish problem"*? Yes. Does the document of Romans 9-11 comprise all we have in the pages of the NT scriptures about *the who?* No.

Another writer, one who never identified himself, penned a "word of exhortation" (Hebrews 13:22) to prepare and empower those who lived in the shadow of the Temple. He feared that they might become intimated, deceived, and overwhelmed by the Zionistic Nationalism that enjoyed a renaissance during the 60s.

This unknown author strongly felt that they stood in imminent danger. He believed that they needed to "take care, lest there be in any of you an evil, unbelieving heart, leading you to fall away from the living God... (3:12-15). These Hebrew Christians lived in a situation facing a make-or-break time of crisis.

Several components came together to make this a crisis time for them. First, Jewish Nationalism had experienced a rejuvenation. With the Zealot movement at its zenith, an air of messianic expectancy spread everywhere among the Jews. As the Zealot movement reached its zenith, Jewish fundamentalism experienced a renewal. Zealotism resurged and energized Jerusalem, Palestine, and the Jewish centers throughout the empire. Visions of once again becoming a free and independent nation arose in the hearts of the people.

Second, this induced doubts in many believers. "If the messiah has already come, then why do we still live as an oppressed people under the Romans?" With the resurgence of Judaism, some entertained thoughts of quitting. They entertained the idea of quitting and returning to Judaism.

Third, a power of deception worked among them. They felt inferior as a minority group up against the strong and vibrant Jewish Renaissance. The Jews rather than treating the Jesus believers as equals, they viewed them as misfits and renegades to the Hebrew faith.

Nor could those who gave allegiance to the Nazareth prophet really join the resurgence. They believed the messiah had already come, that the gentle prophet had already brought in the new day, and that he would return to complete it within their lifetime. Yet, day by day they lived in the thriving and bustling Zealotism that talked about the restored Davidic kingdom. Metropolis Jerusalem became more and more charged with this kind of excitement. Everybody felt nervous. Would they go to war? Would the Davidic messiah soon appear? This stood as the cultural atmosphere permeating every Jewish center around the Mediterranean.

With all this fundamentalism fervor, some believers became fainthearted for the old ways. It tried their souls. They felt "zealous for the law" and yet aware that Christianity transcended such nationalism. Some actually turned their backs on the crucified messiah and opted for a warrior messiah. Instead of "going out of the camp" to Jesus, they chose the Zealot hope (Heb. 6:1-6). Others slowly drifted away, no longer attending the meetings (2:1-4, 10:24-25).

The presence of the Temple, the priesthood, the daily sacrifice, the Torah served as too much for many of them. They began to doubt. They questioned the "glory" of the new covenant; the old one seemed so much more glorious. No wonder the unknown author wrote *Hebrews* as a "word of exhortation" to shake them up and solidify their faith for the end of that age.

The text of *Hebrews* elegantly and profoundly presents the reality of Jesus and the supremacy of his new covenant (ch. 1), the supremacy of his priesthood over the Aaron priesthood of the Levites (ch. 2,5,7), his deliverance into the new promise land of rest (sabbath) (4), the wonder and power of the new eternal covenant (7-10), and final sacrifice (8-10,13).

The author's main point focused on Jesus. He argued succinctly, powerfully, and rabbinically that they should attend to Jesus "the apostle and high priest of our confession" (3:1, 8:1-2).

Further, saturated with OT references and symbols, this document highlights Jesus as it warns of a judgment day that "was drawing near" (10:25). This soon to come judgment day would bring an end to the old, and simultaneously destroy God's opponents. And that day (August 22, 70 AD) occurred when the Temple burned to the ground after "the Abomination of Desolation" stood in the holy place. This brought an end to the holy place, the Jewish Age, the priesthood, sacrifices, capital, genealogies, etc.

THE END-TIME BOOK OF HEBREWS

Spiritually, the author discovered that his Hebrew recipients had fallen into some tough coping times. These believers had become "dull of hearing" and sluggish in spirit (5:11-14, 6:12). They felt discouraged; they suffered from "faintness of mind," so that they begun to "shrink back" from their faith (12:1-2, 10:39). Disheartened, they began to fail to endure (10:35). What in the world set off such poor coping?

Time (their sense of "time"). When they gave allegiance to Jesus, their "hope" rested in the fulfillment of the new covenant, and the full glory of the new covenant age. But now almost forty years later, it had not yet occurred. Nor had Jesus' words about the end, occurring in their generation, transpired. In fact, nothing radically had changed in Israel since the coming of the new covenant on Pentecost. Further, Judaism seemed stronger than ever! What does this renewed Zionism mean?

Do you find it any wonder then that they found it tough to live as a Christian when so very little had changed in Israel since they believed? Yet shortly everything would change. Soon their entire world would end. That which God had designed as old *"is becoming obsolete and growing old is ready to vanish away"* (8:13). "For yet a little while, and the coming one shall come and shall not tarry..." (10:37). Something big and dangerous and yet wonderful stood on the horizon; "the Day" drew nearer and nearer (10:25).

JESUS --THE END-DAY PROPHET
Hebrews 1

As *Hebrews* opens *it pinpoints the when, what and why*. "In these last days (when), God has spoken to us by a Son (what)... Therefore we must pay the closer attention to what we have heard, lest we drift away from it" (1:2, 2:1). Because "the world to come, of which we are speaking" was not subjected to angels, but to the son (why) (2:5).

In this biblical context, the "last days" refer to those of the old covenant. "God spoke of old to our fathers by the prophets, but *in these last days* he has spoken to us by a Son..." (1:1-2). The days which that author wrote comprised the "last days" of the covenant wherein people looked to "the Law and the Prophets" (Isa. 8:20) for God's authoritative message. But now (AD 64) in ("these last days"), God had created a new way of talking, i.e. through his son. Son-communications has now replaced prophet communications.

The author used a rabbinical argument to prove the superiority of Jesus over angels (1:3-14). Why angels? To follow this you now need to shift your thinking to think Hebraically. Answer: because *God delivered the old covenant by angels* (Heb. 2:2, Acts 7:38, Gal. 3:12). "Angel" in this chapter refers to the old covenant (just as "death" does in II Cor. 3:7).

This son holds a special relation and uniqueness. He "reflects the glory of God" (the Temple's Shekinah of glory), "bears the very stamp of his nature" and "upholding the universe by his word of power" (1:3). Does this underscore his importance or what? This son came into the world, "made purification for sins," and then God crowned him king. All this underscores that the end has come to the old, and that a new world would shortly arise in its fullness.

In Hebrews one, the author portrays Jesus as *the world-changer*. God brought the old world (age, i.e. Mosaic dispensation) into existence through Jesus (1:2,10). In these last days, he would bring that world to an end, rolling them up like a mantle so that "they will be changed" (1:12). (Do you now find yourself getting the hang of thinking Hebraically? If you find it tough, read the Psalms; that will help.)

THE CHRISTIAN AGE
"The World to Come of Which We Speak"
Hebrew 2

At the end of the old Jewish world ("these last days," 1:2), some world-changing events would shortly occur to wrap things up (8:13). This would transpire very shortly (10:37) because the change of covenants would become ompleted.

Formerly God dealt with men with his *angel-ordained Torah* and communicated via his prophets in various ways and times. But no longer. "In these last days" he had begun to use *a son-ordained covenant* and son-communication method. The superiority of this new *more excellent* method rested in this son radiating God's very glorious (Shekinah) person (1:3), and accomplishing what the old covenant could not--"purification for sins" (1:4).

After this transcendence and specialness of Christ, the writer spoke about his flesh-and-blood humanity. Jesus exists now as the one who we see. "The world to come of which we are speaking" (2:5,9) relates to him and his fulfillment of the prophets. For the prophets had declared that God would bring an end to the old age and bring in a new heavens and earth. "The world to come, of which we speak" refers to *the world of prophet declaration* about the coming of the Messiah.

The full completion of this new world would see "man" and "the son of man" (Psalm 8) "crowned with glory and honor" with "everything in subjection under his feet" (2:5-8). This messianic hope in Christ also identifies the very hope of Israel.

In 64 AD, this completion of the old had not yet fully occurred. "We do not yet see everything in subjection to him" (2:8). Currently, "we see Jesus..." crowned with glory and honor because of the cross-event, tasting death for all (2:9), made perfect through suffering (2:10), having shared in flesh-and-blood (2:14), ready to destroy the devil's power of death (2:15), and God's merciful and faithful high priest (2:17). This served as the vision of faith.

The exhortation? *Consider Jesus*, the apostle and high priest of our confession" (3:1). Why? Because he, as "the coming one," will very shortly come and "shall not tarry" (10:37-39). He will completely "shake not only the earth but also heaven" so that "the removal of what is shaken" (the old covenant from Zion, 12:27) will occur and "that which cannot be shaken may remain" (the new covenant).

This argument says that God has now in these last days initiated a whole new covenant through a son by means of his salvation events (cross, resurrection). Shortly, he will bring this new covenant to a completion by returning a second time to judge Judaism and Jerusalem (the AD 70 catastrophe). Then, that which "is becoming obsolete and growing old" will "vanish away" (8:13).

BEING THE NEW GLORIOUS TEMPLE
Hebrews 3

The good-news for the believers in that transitional age consisted of this: "We are [exist as] his [Christ's] house [i.e. Temple], *if* we hold fast our confidence and pride in our hope firm to *the end*" (3:6). But a present danger then existed. It involved hardening the heart via deception ("falling away from the living God" 3:7,12). "For we share in Christ, *if* only we hold our first confidence firm to the end..." (3:15).

What *end* do these verses refer to? **The end of the Jewish world.** But just like Israel under Moses, they now lived in a transitional time between freedom from slavery (Egypt) and entering the promise land. The writer develops this analogy through Chapters three and four.

A scary fact faced first-century Israel. Namely, most of ancient Israel in the wilderness under Moses did not make it. Why? Because they did not pay attention or exhort each other during the period of transition. Subsequently, they fell in the wilderness. And just as they did not leave Egypt and immediately walk into the promised land, a similar situation stood before the early Christian movement.

The "perfect" world of the new covenant did not come at Pentecost. First there came a transitional age--and a "wilderness" time. The Hebrew writer's use of *the transitional wilderness time* paralleled the similar dangers between the church in the wilderness with the first century situation (3:15-19). Though they had already "tasted the powers of the world to come" (6:5), and though this new age of Christ had already started, and though it would shortly become completed, the completion had "not yet" come. So the blessings (including "sabbath rest") described had not come in its fullness.

ENDURING THE INTERIM PERIOD
Hebrews 4

In the case of Israel in Egyptian captivity, Moses rescued them from that death and bondage and then lead them, for what should have only involved a three month trek in the wilderness. Yet what should have only taken a few months ended up taking 40 years. Why?

They did not hold good faith with God. Rather, they grumbled and complained. Consequently, out of their unfaithful responses, they doomed themselves to **a forty year interim period** in the wilderness (Numbers 13-14). God swore to those unbelievers, "You will never enter my rest" (Psalm 95:7, Heb. 3:11). He refused to take them into the promise land with an unbelieving attitude. So, they "fell in the wilderness" (3:18). "The good word was not united in faith in the hearers" (4:2), so a transition period of 40 years.

Most significantly, the Hebrew writer used this story to the Hebrew church in Jerusalem as the old age drew to a close. The end of another 40 year interim period would soon end. The interim period between the covenants that spanned the time from the cross (Jesus' death) to his parousia ("coming" or "presence") in the Jerusalem judgment on Judaism would soon occur.

Would history repeat itself? Would first-century Israel conclude things as their forefathers had begun? Would they let unbelief, not listening, and not integrating their faith cause them also to "fall in the wilderness?" The Hebrew writer prayed it would not. So he wrote his exhortations. "While the promise of entering his rest remains, let us fear lest any of you be judged to have failed to reach it" (4:1).

This falling *cannot* have reference to their ultimate salvation. Why? Because God's gift of eternal life comprises just that--a gift. That means it does not function in a conditional way: "Maybe you have it, maybe you don't." Paul made this clear: "*There is no condemnation* for those who are in Christ Jesus" (Romans 8:1). "The gift of God is eternal life through Jesus Christ our Lord" (Romans 6:23).

How should we understand this "falling?" As the falling that would occur among those new covenant people who would not see the new era come in its fullness. They stood on the verge of seeing the completion ("the perfect") come (I Cor. 13:8-13). The old covenant stood ready to vanish away (8:13), and the "time of reformation" had come (9:10). A "rest" awaited them as the ultimate "promise land," the "sabbath rest for the people of God" (4:9). "Let us therefore strive to enter that rest, that no one fall by the same sort of disobedience" (4:11).

Would they make the transition from the old world to the new world? Jesus had already spied out the new world. As the "pioneer" of their salvation, he had blazed the trail for them. Would they get scared about the giants in the land? Would they see themselves as grasshoppers in their own eyes compared to the external features of the old covenant? Would they "go forth to him outside the camp" (13:13)? Would they look to "Jesus the pioneer and perfecter of our faith" (12:2)? They could not fool him about it. "Before him no creature is hidden, but all are open and laid bare to the eyes of him with whom we have to do" (4:13).

MOVING PAST 'LAST THINGS'
Hebrews 5-6

To the Hebrew believers Jesus came as God's "last days" prophet. He came to deliver the final word about the new world (the new covenant), which would shortly come in its fullness. Accordingly, he functioned as the pioneer of this great salvation. As the son over God's temple of which they existed as a part, they needed to persevere. "If we hold fast our profession firm to the end." Jesus would function as the new Joshua bringing them into the final and ultimate sabbath "rest" if they would mix with faith the good word they had heard from him.

All these conditional words did not refer to their relational salvation with God. It referred to them entering *the promise land of the new covenant world* that would soon come. Would they become a part of the community who would enter that new experience?

If they would, they would have to not "drift away" from spiritual development, or live only on milk. They must not remain "unskilled in the word of righteousness" (5:13). That would disempower them from "going on to maturity." They needed to "leave the elementary doctrine of messiah." Those "first principles of God's word" served only as the foundation. Do you consider these only foundational principles?

> *Repentance from dead works*
> *Faith toward God*
> *Instruction about ablutions (baptisms)*
> *Laying on of hands*

The resurrection of the dead
Eternal Judgment

First principles? Yes! To the Hebrew author, these simply consisted of *elementary facets* which the recipients needed to *leave* so that they could move on to more mature things! Today many consider repentance (changing the mind), faith (trust), and baptism as basic. Some might even consider ordination ("laying on of hands") basic. But resurrection and eternal judgment? How do these function as basic and foundational? How could we leave these things and move on to something else?

If these comprise things to build on and to move on from, these must simply express the basic gospel truths. They must consist of truths like in Christ we "do not come into judgment, but have passed from death into life" (John 5:24). In him, the firstfruit (of the first believers) have already raised to walk in newness and life and shall shortly become fully raised (Rom. 6). In other words, *the new world* has already started to arrive and its completeness would soon become consummated. They did not have to wait around to taste the powers of the world to come; the kingdom had already broken into the human experience and would soon complete that inbreaking.

INTERIM COVENANT "APOSTASY"
Hebrews 6

If you have followed by checking the references in your Bible, you will now notice the number, intensity, and frequency of the apostasy warnings in *Hebrews*. The form and expression of this apostasy comprised a very special kind. We should not confuse it with what we call backsliding. Dull boredom did not consist of their temptation ("Oh I'm just sick of church and want to do something more inspirational on the weekend").

The "apostasy" the author addressed comprised a more deadly and toxic kind. It involved "crucifying the Son of God on their own account and holding him up to contempt" (6:6). Now that involves something very different from not attending church.

Actually, many of the Hebrews had already backslidden in terms of attendance. They already showed their laziness, drifting, immaturity, dullness of hearing, and not attending regularly (Heb. 10:25). Yet they had not committed the apostasy that the author so feared for them.

The apostasy the writer spoke about consisted of something that went far beyond merely giving up "the good things of the world to come" (6:4-5). It involved *repudiating* those powers and experiences and *rejecting* the new covenant blessings.

This passage therefore addresses *covenant apostasy* then. This explains the presence of the covenant curses (6:7-8, Deut. 27-28). If they turned their backs on "the pioneer of their faith," the "apostle and high priest of the great salvation," the person through whom God spoke and worked in those last days --they would not become part of the transitional community that would go into "the new world." Like the pilgrims from Egypt under Moses, they would not get to go into the promise land.

Judaism, the threat and scourge of that day, had served its purpose and would soon "vanish away" (Heb. 8:13). But if anyone rejected the Messiah and turned back to the old, they would essentially turn back to *"dead" works* and a kingdom that God would soon shake up.

Solution? "Hold firm your confidence and pride of hope firm to the end" (3:6, 14). "To show the same earnestness in realizing the full assurance of hope until the end" (6:11). The writer wanted them to become proactive by getting off their rear-ends. That time had become crucial. They had no time for drifting mindlessly. "In realizing full assurance" --actualize your hope. Trust it and commit yourself to it. "Full assurance of hope" in the promises of the new world coming in its completion.

To induce a state of assurance and "anchor" their souls into God's reality (6:13-19), the writer zoomed back to the "oath" God swore to Abraham (Gen. 12:1-3, Gal. 3:8). Thinking covenantally, he asserted that there existed "two unchangeable things" (the oath and the swearing) that provide "strong consolation," a "refuge," a "sure and steadfast anchor of the soul." *The oath* said, "Blessing, I will bless you..." *The swearing* comprised God's style of communication; he "swore" the blessing, thus pledging it upon his own immutable self.

"Men swear by a greater than themselves, and in all their disputes an oath is final for confirmation" (6:16). God did the same thereby giving them confirmation. God wrapped the heart of the gospel's new covenant promises in a sworn oath so that now "we have this as a sure and steadfast anchor of the soul, a hope that enters into the inner shrine behind the curtain..." (6:19).

THE AGE-CHANGING COVENANT
Hebrews 7

The *Hebrews* writer viewed his priesthood chapter as something "hard to be interpreted" (5:11). He expected that it would demand his first-century readers to use their teeth since he planned to give them some "meat of the word" that would demand chewing (5:12-14). In so doing, he hoped that their faculties would become trained to distinguish good (teaching) from evil (5:14). In so doing, he argued using a rabbinical form of reasoning to convey his evangelical message.

The heart of his message? The covenants would soon change--completely and finally. "There is a change in the priesthood" which "necessitates a change in the law as well" (7:12).

The new Christian age would bring about a change of the Levitical priesthood. David had prophesied that the lord who would sit at God's right hand would rule his people in the day of his power and would become "a priest for ever after the order of Melchizedek" (Psalm 110:1-4). For so had God sworn in an oath. Now if the messiah exists as a "great high priest" after the order of Melchizedek, this eliminates all Levitical priests and priesthood. Why? Because theirs represents an inferior and less effective priesthood.

In covenant history, priest and king Melchizedek blessed Abraham by ministering to him when he used sacramental items (bread and wine) (Gen. 14:17-20). A thousand years later, David said the messiah would become one after the Melchizedek model.

What conclusion can we draw from this? "What further need would there have been for another priest to arise after the order of Melchizedek, rather than one named after the order of Aaron---*if* perfection had been attainable through the Levitical priesthood" (7:11)?

His question functions rhetorically. It says in effect, "There would arise no need!" God promised that a change would come in the new age; Jesus came bringing in the beginning of this new era. This means that no one could attain *"perfection"* under the Levitical priesthood. Yet, under that priesthood "the people received the Law" (7:11). Conclusion? *"When there is a change in the priesthood, there is necessarily a change in the law as well"* (7:12). Bingo! God will now change the law (or covenant arrangement).

The great difference about the priesthoods arises from the fact that a Melchizedek priest does not arise (becomes operative) by genealogy ("bodily descent"). His inward authenticity arises "by the power of an indestructible life" (7:16). A mighty high standard! A priest after this model has to personally partake in the new covenant "life" (eternal life) so he can "continue for ever" (7:24).

"The law made nothing perfect" (7:19) explains the need for a new covenant and priesthood. In this sense, the old comprises a process characterized by weakness and uselessness. The process of people made "perfect" in this context refers to the ability/right of one to "draw near to God" (7:19). And this illustrates the power of Jesus' priesthood; he "saves them who draw near to God to the uttermost" (7:25). He "always lives to make intercession for them." And because of his "once for all" offering, he perfectly initiates a reconciled relationship with God.

With a new priesthood that effectively accomplishes what old could not, this necessitates a change of the law. The old covenant has proved ineffective, impotent, and useless. So the time had come, in these last days of the Judaic world, for God to initiate *a new covenant* with his people (the thematic focus of chapters

8-10).

THE NEW WORLD OF THE NEW COVENANT
Hebrews 8

Covenant history via the nation of Israel effectively demonstrated the failure of law to make men whole. Torah turned out as a weak and useless force; "the law made nothing perfect" (7:18). Accordingly, Jeremiah (among others), prophesied that *God would make a new covenant with Israel* (Jer. 31:31-34). He foresaw the last days of the old covenant coming when God would initiate a new process of **perfection** (i.e. a "drawing near to God"). God would base this *on a better hope* than that of law (7:19).

Something excelling the old Torah Covenant would come to Israel at the end. "Christ has obtained a ministry which is as *much more excellent than the old* as the covenant he mediates is better, since it is enacted on *better promises*" (8:6). The new would excel the Temple of Solomon, the rituals, the priesthood, etc. because it would operate, in nature and promise, as a much greater covenant. How specifically would this superiority show itself?

The linguistic construction of Hebrews 8 plays off the terminology *"But now..." better covenant* (8:6). The writer said, "for if the first covenant has been faultless, there would have been no occasion for a second..." He then listed the **differences**. This challenges us to see the differences that Jeremiah and the *Hebrews* writer highlighted. Over-generalizing, discounting the differences, not recognizing the shifts and changes fails to catch the significance these writers sought to present.

The terminology used here asserts: *"not like..." "not according to..."* (ou kata ten diatheken, 8:9). The divine Godly covenant with Israel, 1400 BC differs from the divine Godly covenant with the world via Christ, 30 AD. The "same" covenant-making God offering each--but a "new" covenant different from, "not according to...", the old covenant. Hebrews 8, in fact, **specifies how** the new differs from the old.

(1) God would make the new covenant *internal* in location. "I will put my laws into their minds and write them on their hearts" (8:10). Its newness would consist of something internal--a phenomenon of consciousness. Unlike the old external covenant/kingdom, the new would be "within" (Luke 17:20-21). The externality of the old made that kingdom tangible in all of its features. The new consists of something "of the spirit" (spiritual), hence of the person (Rom. 12:1-2).

(2) God would make the new covenant *personal and relational*. "I will be to them a God, and they shall be my people" (8:10). What a contrast with the legal-ritual old covenant! The new involves an "I-Thou" relation, not an impersonal standing mediated by law ("I-it"). Unlike law-relationships which function as rule-driven, personal relationships operate as love-driven. The first involves the letter of the law, the second, the spirit of the law (II Cor. 3:4-6).

(3) God would make it *experiential*. "They shall not teach... saying 'Know the Lord,' they shall know me" (8:11). The old functioned by law. This meant that the children *born into it* would then have to receiving taught about their covenant God. In the new, people become "born" into it by means of their experiential knowing and experiencing of God. "Knowing" God through the person of Jesus comprises the very means of experiencing and entering his reign.

(4) God would make it an effectively *gracious and healing* covenant. "I will be merciful toward their iniquities, and I will remember their sins no more" (8:12). Experiencing the new world means experiencing total forgiveness in a relationship of grace. This itself functions as a healing experience.

These *better promises* of the new covenant lead to its "much more excellent ministry." These components distinguish the old from the new. The old comprised something external, literal, legal, and impersonal whereas the new involves something spiritual, internal, personal, and experiential. To the extent a person doesn't know how to make these **covenant distinctions**, to that extent, a person will probably lack the ability to see the kingdom. This gives us insight into why the *Hebrews* writer presented this to his readers.

THE TWO WORLDS
One Unreal/ The Other Very Real
Hebrews 9

The furniture, items, actions, rituals, etc. of the old covenant served merely as "a copy and *shadow* of the heavenly sanctuary" (8:5). The old covenant worship regulations existed as "symbolic for the present age" (the old covenant time) "until the time of reformation" (9:10) (the new covenant time). "Since the law (torah) has but *a shadow* of the good times to come instead of the *true form* of these realities..." (10:1).

Question. How much reality do you give to a shadow? Imagine the shadow of one of your loved ones. How close, bonded, or intimate could you interact with that shadow? How sane would we judge you if you spent more time and energy dealing with the shadow than the reality that casts that shadow? Could the shadow of your car take you anywhere? Would that shadow serve any useful function for anything? Yet this describes precisely what some of the Hebrews Christians did in essence as they over-valued the shadows of the old world. (see Appendix A--Shadows)

Don't get me wrong; shadows do have important purposes. If I see a shadow coming upon me as I walk down a sidewalk on a late afternoon, I can appreciate the shadow's informational signaling power. The message of that shadow may save my life. Sometimes I even hunt for shadows. When I have hiked in the desert in the heat of a cloudless day, times have occurred when I have desperately wanted the coolness and relief in the shadow of a cliff. Such shadows do not exist without value. They do serve highly valuable services.

Yet ultimately, *shadow and reality* comprise two different kinds of "realities;" each having its own nature, function, and value. Problems arise when we fail to distinguish them. The inability to make such distinctions initiates *unsanity* because it prevents us from making a good adjustment to reality.

This describes the case for some in the Hebrew Church. They continued to confuse shadow with substance. In their mix-up they looked on the "earthly" sanctuary as the real thing, and the new heavenly/spiritual sanctuary as the shadow. *Not!*

Christian truth made this clear. "*The law has but a shadow* of the good things to come *instead of the true form* of these realities" (10:1). Similarly: "Questions of food and drink...festival or new moon or a sabbath ...are *only a shadow* of what is to come; but the substance belongs to Christ" (Col. 2:16-17).

The reality of the heavenly Jerusalem of the new world involves something intangible and spiritual. Comprising the nature of spirit, and not flesh, God has written it within the heart, not on external things like stones or paper and ink. The new sanctuary exists within the very minds-hearts of believers. That speaks about **where** Christ as high priest ministers his "new and living way" (10:19). The new covenant's reality comprises the substance that the old covenant only foreshadowed.

WHEN THE OLD COVENANT WORLD ENDED
Hebrews 9-10

Christ "has appeared once for all *at the end of the age* to put away sin by the sacrifice of himself" (9:26). This good-news occurred at the end of the old covenant world. The world of Torah had not proven itself to serve as good-news to its people. It did **not** bring the blessing of Abraham either to the Jews nor to the Gentiles. It did not even consist of the "real" thing, but merely functioned as "a shadow of the good things to come instead of the true form of these realities..." (10:1).

This explains why the old world had to end. (The old world did **not** end because the Jewish nation rejected their messiah!) God had to take "the former commandment" and "set [it] aside because of its weakness and uselessness (for the law made nothing perfect) on the other hand, a better hope is introduced through which we draw near to God" (7:18-19).

This new covenant world *began* at the first coming (with Christ's birth, ministry, cross, and resurrection) (it began to come into the world). Jesus "entered, not into a sanctuary made with hands, a copy of the true one, but into heaven itself, now to appear in the presence of God on our behalf" (9:24). This perfect appearing presented a once-for-all sacrifice that brought redemption. If it did not, "he would have had to suffer repeatedly since the foundation of the world" (i.e. the foundation of the new Christian world, 9:26).

What reality brings the good things? **The new covenant.** In it Jesus offered what we could not give the Father, perfect obedience to God's will (10:5-10). So Jesus offered that very thing and thereby initiated *a whole new world*. In this new era we can now confidently enter the sanctuary by "a new and living way" (10:19-20) and "draw near with a true heart in full assurance of faith," hearts cleansed, bodies washed (10:21-22). This then brings a whole new world of *new covenant resources* into our lives (10:19-25).

Now in 64 AD, the believers lived in the transitional days of the interface between the old and new covenants. During this time God slowly changed the covenants over a period of forty years. Consequently, the covenant curses described in this text applied to those of that transitional age who lived during the time of the change. They might shrink back to destruction (10:26-39).

"The Day drawing near" would occur "yet a little while, and the Coming One shall come and shall not tarry" (10:25, 37). The furious and fearful judgment upon Judaism would then come upon them when the abomination of desolation (the Romans armies) would "consume the adversaries."

Such apostasy would bring a more severe judgment than Moses' law (10:26-29). How about that! I would have thought that these people did not live "under law but under grace" (Romans 6:14-15)? But no. They wanted to live under law. And given that desire and presupposition, the writer ran with it and showed them what that would mean (compare Gal. 5:2-12). To go back to law indicates just how far they had fallen for the seduction of going back to the shadow. To do such essentially meant to repent of their allegiance to Christ, to "spurn the Son of God, to profane the blood of the covenant, and to outrage the spirit of grace" (10:29). No wonder such actions would make them enemies to the cross (10:31). If they wanted to live as God's covenant people they must live by faith, hang on to their confidence and endure to the end of the old (10:32-39).

THE FAITH-RISK OF LEAVING THE OLD WORLD
Hebrews 11

If you know that Hebrews 11 focused on faith, what consists of *the context* of that chapter's faith challenge? If we contextualize it to members of the Hebrew Church prior to the fall of Jerusalem, we then understand *the specific object* in which the author called them to believe.

The answer in context refers to the line just prior to Chapter 11. Namely, *"the Coming One shall come and shall not tarry."* For "yet a very little while" (10:37) and the judgment day would arrive. The "Day was drawing near" (10:26) which would bring that judgment in a fury of fire, etc. (10:26-31).

What does this mean? Namely that God currently wanted them to *apply their eyes of faith and see something spiritual*--the end of the old covenant world, the end of Judaism. This now explains why the writer affirmed that faith consists of the belief and assurance of "things hoped for" (i.e. the new world of Christ's new covenant). This "conviction" of things not seen (11:1) would enable them to hold on to "in full assurance of faith" (10:22). It would empower them to "hold faith and keep their souls" (10:39), rather than shrink back to destruction.

Such faith "understands that the world (i.e. the new covenant world) was created by the word of God (through Jesus), so that what is seen was made out of things which do not appear" (11:3). Lots of people literalize these words. Yet to literalize these verses to the creation of the planet means that one has forgotten to notice the immediate context which speaks about *covenant*. It means that one forgets the basic Christian principle that we walk, not by sight, but by faith (II Cor. 5:7).

The Son-Communication that God initiated in "the last days"

(Heb. 1:1-3) had brought "the word of God" that created a new world (ch. 1). No wonder the object of their faith focused on the pioneer and perfecter of their faith, Jesus (12:2). So to him they needed to look to and consider lest they "grow weary or fainthearted" (12:3).

Then they would have the confidence and courage to "go forth to him outside the camp..." (13:13). It takes faith to journey out from old familiar camps. In those days it took real faith to believe that God had created a new thing in the world as he had promised. And precisely because the old kingdom would shortly become shaken and removed (12:27), they needed faith to "receive a kingdom that cannot be shaken" (12:28).

Now the list of faith-heroes in Hebrews 11 provides story after story about faith-people in Hebrew history who moved out, "not knowing where they were going," but who trusted that God's word provided them a more solid reality than the external and material things that they could see, hear, and feel.

Such faith takes risks and engages in the challenge. Such faith operates as a function of courage. Such faith had showed up in Hebrew history as in Abel offering, Enoch walking, Noah building, Abraham traveling and offering up Isaac, Isaac invoking, Jacob blessing, Joseph foreseeing, Moses refusing, leaving, sprinkling, the Israelites walking, Rahab welcoming, etc. In all of these sacred stories of faith, the conviction and assurance of faith as a "title-deed" to the future provided a way for those faith-pioneers to mentally chart out their direction in response to God's call. In context, this list of Hebrew fathers of faith would have powerfully pulled on their heart-strings.

Bonhoeffer (1937/1970) in *"The Cost of Discipleship"* talked about situations that arise which *make faith possible*. Some people call these situations "problems." Others curse them as satanic and construct their lives so they have fewer and fewer situations where faith "is made possible." Their "security moves" eliminates the need for *the courage to risk*. They plan, insure, and protect themselves from moving out not knowing where they go. They accept no challenge for stretch. And because they settle for the status quo, they needed no "title-deed" to the future.

Yet others learn to "walk by faith, not by sight." They hear the voice of God calling, accept the risk of moving out, walk on water, build arks in deserts, sacrifice short-term pleasures for the possibility of a whole new destiny. In the tradition of Hebrew storytelling, Hebrews 11 packages the risk of faith in the adventure of these faith-heroes. To understand this chapter--*memorize the verbs*. They "through faith conquered kingdoms, enforced justice, received promises, stopped the mouths of lions, quenched raging fire, escaped the edge of the sword, won strength out of weakness, became mighty in war, put foreign armies to flight..." (11:34).

What does this all say, in context, to the believers in AD 64? Use your faith in the Jewish Messiah to go out not knowing where you go, trusting God's word as the ultimate reality, and risking yourselves to the word of his grace. Stop trusting your physical sight in the old covenant, in Judaism, and in the shadows of the old. The new has come and "the coming one" will again shortly come to bring a completion, so trust him to the very end.

DEVELOPING THE FAITH
TO AUTHENTICALLY ENTER THE NEW WORLD
Hebrews 11

Accepting that the old world ended and the new world began necessitates authentic faith. This means thinking in a new way. It means holding ideas about the "things hoped for" as desired outcomes and then treating them as real--as potentially real (11:1). It then means acting on those unseen reality beliefs.

Many stop with just intellectual faith. They "believe that God exists" (11:6). They mentally hold the "conviction of things not seen," but it stops there. It doesn't move them to take effective action.

To become the authentic thing, faith must transform to *faith-living*. True believers get involved; they actively seek after the God who "rewards those who seek him." They *actively respond* to the word of faith like Abraham who responded trustingly and became *a spiritual explorer* par excellence

(11:8-19). "He went out, not knowing where he was to go." His sojourn in the land of promise involved living in tents with Isaac and Jacob, never receiving the promise, but looking forward to "the city which had foundations, whose builder and maker is God" (11:10).

Upon hearing the voice of God, he began responding. Could that heard "voice" exist as part of his hopes and dreams? Probably. Childless Abraham and Sarah wanted children. After the voice said they would have children "as innumerable as the sand by the seashore" came the test of faith. How did they experience that test? In their daily, weekly, monthly, yearly attempts to have children. Yet, for them, they only met with failure after failure. Year after laborious year passed with no children in sight. Perhaps no real voice spoke to them. Perhaps the word did not consist of anything authentic. They could have given up.

But Abraham and Sarah didn't; they kept believing. They kept acting and relating on that trusted voice. "I have made you the father of many nations." Now trusting that word when they got into their 90s, well.... They believed in him "who gives life to the dead and calls into existence the things that do not exist. In hope Abraham believed against hope, that he should become the father of many nations" (Romans 4:16-18).

> "He did not weaken in faith when he considered his own body, which was as good as dead because he was about a hundred years old, or when he considered the barrenness of Sarah's womb. No distrust made him waver concerning the promise of God, but he grew strong in his faith as he gave glory to God, fully convinced that God was able to do what he had promised" (4:19-21).

For Abraham and Sarah, the act of faith involved *making love*. Pretty radical stuff, wouldn't you say?! Isaac, after all, did not come into existence through a virgin birth. He resulted from an old man and an old women who took God at his word and kept behaving as if that word existed as the most real thing in the world.

So "Sarah herself received power to conceive..." *Authentic faith acts by moving out into the new world that God creates.* Contextually, the Hebrew writer challenged the members of the Jerusalem Church to move out to the scary unknowns of things unseen --the end of the old world.

DEVELOPING FAITH THAT ENDURES THE TRIBULATION
Hebrews 12

Hebrews 11 may seem like a survey of biblical history. But that misunderstands that chapter. The author did *not* write it to inform. Israel had long know all that information. Rather than history, those faith-heroes who "went through hell," and yet hung-in and endured, comprised members of the old covenant age that would shortly end. And they all "died in faith *not* having received what was promised" (11:13).

Abel suffered the hatred that lead to his murder, Abraham with Isaac and Jacob "sojourned in the land of promise living in tents," Moses failed to enter the promised land, others "suffered mocking and scourging, even chains and imprisonment" (11:36). In fact, the last line of Hebrews 11 asserts, "all these, though well attested by their faith, *did not receive what was promised."*

Endurance expresses the author's theme in this section (10:32 through 12:3). *"You have need of endurance...* for yet a very little while, and the Coming One shall come and shall not tarry" (10:36-7). "Let us *run with perseverance* the race that is set before us..." (12:2).

The author mentioned the faith-heroes solely as *models* for developing the spiritual resource they needed --an enduring faith. What they needed more of all concerned a faith that would not quit. They needed to develop patience, to longsuffer, and to not shrink back in their faith. They needed to "hold faith and keep their souls" (10:39) as the days of tribulation would offer them some rough waters to navigate.

The runner who runs a race by constantly changing his objective, his end-goal, will run in circles or run all over the place and never finish "the course set before him." He will expend lots of energy, may even run with great speed, but if he doesn't keep his eyes on the course or on the pace-setting person, he will run like a jackrabbit and get nowhere.

Accordingly, Jesus "the pioneer and perfecter of our faith" has blazed the trail; one that often goes through tough times. "Who for the joy that was set before him endured the cross, despising the shame, and is seated at the right hand of the throne of God" (12:2).

What serves as *the secret for developing an enduring faith?* A new mental focus.

> "**Consider** him who endured from sinners such hostility against himself, so that you may not grow weary or fainthearted" (12:4).

Make this mind-setting perspective your focus by using Jesus as your model of endurance.

Do you have a pattern of impatience, low frustration tolerance, and unwillingness to endure struggles? Then you probably constantly program your mind with ideas like, "Things ought to be easy!" "Why can't I get my way?" To change that programming, use the ideas from the models of Hebrews 11-12 to build empowering beliefs that give you more endurance strength.

EMPOWERMENT RESOURCES FOR COPING WHEN THE WORLD ENDS
Hebrews 12

Given the new world would come by means of God shaking down the old world, the Hebrew church would need much empowerment in order to handle tough times during this time of crisis. Accordingly, the writer called for a new attitude that reframes the old ways of thinking. Then they would not "faint in mind" and become weary (12:3). Such mental fainting would come from mis-perceiving and mis-interpreting their experiences. So the writer offered some enhancing frames-of-references to give them a new way to look at things. He wanted them empowered to persevere, to run the race set before them steadfastly, and to not forget the encouragements (12:1-5).

Shortly, these people would suffer some of Nero's persecutions and then the ravages of the Jewish-Roman War. Times would shortly become very tough for them. No wonder they dabbled with the idea of rejecting Jesus for the resurgence of Zionism. They needed to become *tough-minded believers* as they faced "these last days" when God would change the covenants.

The writer presented a rush of *word pictures* which captivate the mind to new and empowering realities. The pictures move us from "running a race" (casting off every weight and looking to Jesus), to experiencing some trips to the woodshed (becoming "disciplined for a short time" "for our good" so that it can "train" us), to making a pilgrimage out of Babylon (the old Jerusalem of Judaism) to the promise land of joy, to receiving the Patriarch's blessings, if we don't sell our inheritance short for a mess of pottage, to no longer standing at the foot of Mt. Sinai and standing terrified with God's promises, but becoming totally raptured to the top of Mt. Zion, the heavenly Jerusalem, singing and celebrating in festal gathering with the angels, to the earth-shaking events of the restored Jews under Zerubbabel, Ezra, and Nehemiah and the promise of the earth-and-heaven shaking events of the incoming kingdom at the end of the age (Heb. 12).

The believers would become empowered during this transition period *if they stayed mentally clear about where they stood*. When you don't know where you stand (with God), then it becomes very difficult to live in a solid, centered, or stable life. In coping with troubles, knowing where you stand represents a crucial skill. Only then can you think and respond strategically. If you do not know where you stand with what happens or will happen, of what God seeks to accomplish, how would you know how you should respond?

This precisely identifies the writer's point.

> "You have not come to what may be touched... You have come to Mount Zion, to the city of the living God, the heavenly Jerusalem..." (12:18,22).

Where do you stand? Do you live your life as if before blazing Sinai with its severe rules and threatening orders? Where do you invest your hope? Do you hope to fulfill every mandate of the law? Do you hope that Israel as a nation will ascend again? Then welcome to the gloom and doom of the Sinai paragraph (12:18-21).

The liberating end-times truth from this chapter reveals that we do not stand before the source of the old world (Mount Sinai). The true Zionist movement has become a spiritual one: "You have come to Mount Zion..." (12:22-24). The nine-fold description of this place incredibly summarizes the essence of the gospel's good-news and identifies the blessings of the Christian community.

- *Mount Zion*
- *City of the Living God*
- *Heavenly Jerusalem*
- *Innumerable angels in Festal Gathering*
- *Assembly of first-born enrolled in heaven*
- *God the judge*
- *Spirits of just men made perfect*
- *Mediator Jesus of the New Covenant*
- *Gracious speaking sprinkled blood*

What does *the new heavenly Jerusalem* represent? The church of the new covenant! This "the mother of us all" (Gal. 4:21-31) had come and would shortly come into its fullness. Soon they would fully "receive a kingdom that cannot be shaken" (12:28).

Three lines describe it: Mount Zion, City of Living God, heavenly Jerusalem. **Where** does this place exist? In Christ. Three lines describe those **who** lives there: an un-countable party of angels all dancing and singing, all of the resurrected believers (first-born) who God has "enrolled" in heaven, and "spirits" of the just made perfect. Three lines describe the divine side: God who saves by judging all, Jesus who mediates a new covenant by his gracious speaking blood.

This passage provides convincing evidence that the eschatology spoken by Jesus and his apostles involved something that they believed would happen in the first century --the end of the old covenant. That indicates the world that they all expected to end--and which did come to an end. The new world they longed for, and moved toward, consisted of *the new covenant world*. The NT writers Hebraically designated it, "the new heavens and the new earth" wherein would dwell righteousness. This would not bring history or the planet to an end. It would rather begin history in a radically new context: forgiveness, grace, renewal, the power of God's spirit, love, etc.

Now where do you stand with God? Has not Jesus invited you to the top of Mount Zion to dance with the angels in celebration of your enrollment, justification, and completion? Yes, of course!

LIVING IN THE TRANSITION
Hebrews 13

How does one live when the covenants stand in the process of changing? How do you conduct yourself when one of your worlds end? The author provided the following information for those who would live through the transition period of the shift of covenants. Why? Simply to provide them some basic guidelines for coping effectively as the changes get ready to come.

First, do not let your love grow cold (Matt. 24:12-23). "Let brotherly love continue" (13:1) and manifest itself in showing hospitality to strangers (13:2). Show it also in remembering those in prison (13;3) and staying true to your marriage partner (13:4). Nor misdirect your love to a "love of money," but rather learn to become content with what you have; after all, you have God's covenant promise of his sustaining presence (13:5-6).

Obviously, the state of "love" offers a great resource. It offers a very empowering state. Yet love often becomes one of the first things to go when people fall into dire times, experience trials and conflict, etc. Jesus warned about this in his Olivet Apocalypse: "Because wickedness is multiplied, most men's love will grow cold, but he who endures to the end will be saved" (Matt. 24:12-13).

The catastrophe upon them would tempt them to become defensive, ungiving, uncaring, protective, etc. It would dampen their love. The author here instructs them to keep their heart open to strangers, to the imprisoned, to marriage partners, to spiritual values (rather than money). Such love would enable them to "bear all things, hope all things" etc. (I Cor. 13:1-13).

Next, continue to follow your Christian leaders outside the camp of Judaism, bearing the reproach of Jesus (13:7-17). This little paragraph begins and ends with "remember your leaders" and "obey" them. Why? They function as leaders (13:7,17). This means they can help to facilitate and assist others in the process. They have set the pace; they have showed you how to love. "Consider the outcome of their life and imitate their faith." You can tell a true leader by the outcome of their life and faith--they can produce effective actions!

Sandwiched between the leadership verses, the writer speaks about *the change of the covenant.* The externality of the old has given way to the internality of the new. Under the old, the soul could become "strengthened" by "foods" (proper following of the food laws). No longer! Under the new, *souls become strengthened by grace* (13:9). I like that! What a powerful description of the gospel.

Covenantally, the grace of Jesus, forever remains the same (13:8). His lovingkindness holds as steadfast. The old functioned by animal sacrifice, the new by a new alter --Jesus, the Pascal lamb (13:10). The old functioned by the temple made with hands, the new by the gracious blood of Jesus (13:12). The temple has now become internal--within the heart. The old operated by literal and physical sacrifices, the new by the "sacrifice of praise," doing good, and sharing (13:15-16).

In a word, *everything* literal and physical in the old has become **spiritualized** in the new. The old served only a *shadow* of the reality of the new covenant which refers to an internal reality--our person and character in Christ. We now exist as the new Jerusalem (12:22).

This represents an important significance of the fall of Jerusalem and holocaust to fleshly Israel in AD 70. All of the literal and physical aspects of the old covenant gave way to the spiritual and internal aspects of the new. For those who did not know that the world ended, the new covenant came in its completeness, the dead resurrected, eternal life (life and immorality, II Tim. 1:10) came, etc., they keep waiting for "all things to become new."

For those who know, we recognize that with the old waxing

obsolete and ready to vanish away (8:13), a whole new reality came into existence. And that reality has become the current reality.

CONCLUSION

If this exhortation letter to the Hebrews has impressed you--welcome to the club. *Hebrews* represents a tremendous and impactful epistle that not only provides so much of the context of NT eschatology and Hebraic covenant thinking, it functions as an incredibly empowering document. Designed to provide a swift kick to the attitude, the unknown author specified a whole new way of thinking. Here the author articulated the biblical covenant world-view with force and depth. Here we get a sense of "the perfect" (completion) that would soon knock on the door of those original recipients and initiate them into the fullness and completeness of the new covenant that began on Pentecost.

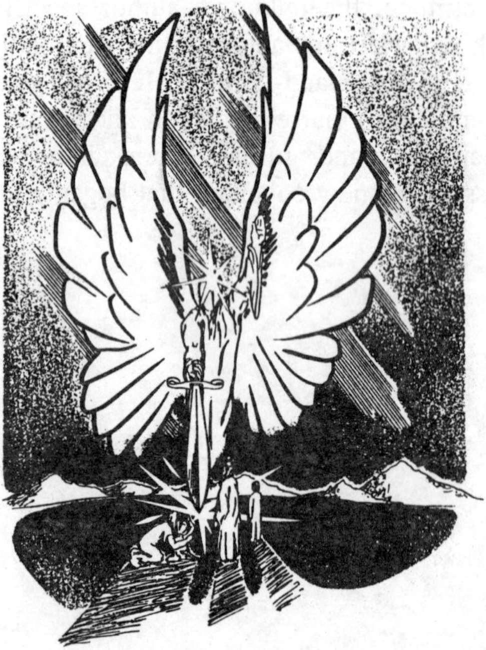

Chapter 7
**

INDEXING THE LITERARY STYLE

"What Kind of Literature Did the Writers Use in Talking about 'the End-of-the-World'?"

The time has come to talk about linguistics. After all, when we *do interpretations*, we inevitably deal with words, language, terms, syntax of language forms, literature, differing types of writing, communicating, languaging, semantics, etc. Only the totally naive would contend that they "take language as it exists," without an awareness that we always engage in interpretation. This simply identifies how the languaging process works.

A number of years ago I met such a person. So naive of the nature and function of language and how it works that like Archy Bunker he asserted with a deity-mode style of talking that he "was the kind of guy who called a spade a spade."

"Oh really!" I responded. "Yes, it means what it says, and that's that!" "So when you talk about a spade, do you have in your mind a shovel kind of a spade or a deck of cards kind of a spade?" Even calling a spade a spade doesn't necessarily settle the reference question!

Crucial to the interpretative science of hermeneutics involves *the kind of literature* a person seeks to understand. What kind of literature does one deal with? We can't get away from the fact that *every genre* of literature necessitates a different set of interpretative principles: poetic principles for poetry, narrative principles for story, exposition principles for essays, etc. By necessity then we must **index the question of style.** "Given this statement that we want to understand with greater clarity in order to discern the original author's meanings, what kind of literature does it represent?" If you have in your hands prose, you will need to handle it in a different way than if you have poetry. You should distinguish parable from mandate, law from gospel, etc.

With regard to the "end of the world" passages throughout the NT, the authors have coded the great majority of them in *a Hebraic literary device called apocalypticism*. John wrote his *Revelation* entirely in this genre. You can also find it scattered throughout the rest of the NT writings. This genre of apocalypticism consisted of the literary style *par excellence* for conveying messages about "the end." Given this, what kind of literature do we have in the apocalyptic? What comprises its characteristics and style?

THE LINGUISTICS OF NT ESCHATOLOGY

Apocalyptic literature and thinking refers to a literature type in vogue from the fourth century BC to the first century AD. In fact, the *zeitgeist* (cultural spirit, spirit of the times) in Jesus' day precisely entailed a highly apocalyptic spirit. This zeitgeist accordingly became the literary style of the NT writers as a kind of "wineskin" for the stormy times that had come upon their world.

Herein lies a danger. If you approach the NT's apocalyptic language without recognizing this genre, and do not know how to deal with its tone, images, and symbols, you will surely misunderstand it and its references. And if you literalize it, you will go very far astray in your understandings! Your ability to handle apocalypticism in *a hermeneutically informed way* then stands as essential to any accurate and intelligent interpretation of the text. Otherwise, you doom your interpretations to inaccuracy and confusion.

THE NATURE OF APOCALYPTICISM
In Its Socio-Political-Religious Context

When we come to the time of the first century, we find apocalypticism in full bloom. By that age many Jewish apocalypses had already arisen and had found ready acceptance. (Many of these you will find still extant, e.g. the Book of Enoch, IV Esdras, Apoc. of Baruch, Sibylline Oracles, etc.). Nor did this literature come to the people of that day as a new literary device. Many of the OT prophets had utilized the apocalyptic style in their oracles (see Isaiah 24-29, Zechariah, Daniel, and Joel 2-3).

You can even find apocalypticism in the *Psalms*. One of my favorite occurs in **Psalm 18**. This Psalm particularly manifests the wild and extravagant extremism so characteristic of apocalypticism. Here David's language and images stretch the imagination as it gives a vision of God's hot nostrils and his supernatural visitation into David's life.

> "The cords of death encompassed me, the torrents of perdition assailed me... In my distress I called upon the Lord; to my God I cried for help. From his temple he heard my voice... Then the earth reeled and rocked; the foundations also of the mountains trembled and quaked, because he was angry. Smoke went up from his nostrils, and devouring fire from his mouth... He bowed the heavens, and came down; thick darkness was under his feet. He rode on a cherub, and flew; he came swiftly upon the wings of the wind..." (Psalm 18:4-15).

Wow! *When* did all that happen? In David's life. Oh really? *How* in the world did it happen in David's time? *In what way?* Look at the actual historical setting given in the Psalm's title: "When God delivered him from his enemies, and from the hand of Saul." Oh really!? I seem to recall God's way of saving David from the hand of Saul in a tad different way (I Samuel 19-31). I don't remember any account about God splitting the heavens and coming down in his cherub chariot! Not literally. Do you?

All this makes a very crucial point that most TV evangelists who appear and talk about eschatology seem to miss. Namely, that if you race into Psalm 18 *literalizing*, if you do not see the figurative use of David's apocalyptic and salvational language, if you seek to make "every word mean strictly what it says," then you will misunderstand the *Psalm*, the spirit of the writing, and come up with all kinds of gross perversions! *To literalize apocalyptic language blinds one to its point.* It also induces one into trying to walk by sight, not by faith. Fortunately, no one that I know of has literalized Psalm 18. Yet the majority of eschatologists, and so-called prophesy experts, literalize the apocalyptic language of the NT writings.

THE SCOOP ABOUT APOCALYPTICISM

Since you will find the language of *Jesus' Short Apocalypse* (Matthew 24), John's long one (*Revelation*), Paul's explanatory one about resurrection (I Cor. 15), etc. coded in apocalyptic language, we need to know about this wild and strange biblical genre.

How well informed do you feel about apocalypticism? How well informed would you like to become? You will do yourself a great favor (even if you never buy the preterist viewpoint) in improving your understanding about this language style so predominant in the Bible. Seek to discover then how the writers utilized it as a literary device for conveying their meanings.

Let's start with its history. *Apocalypticism* arose in Judaism about 200 BC. In this intertestamental time Israel suffered under Greek rule and domination. After their Babylonian captivity (606 BC to 536), they came under Persian rule first and then Greek rule. In the third century B.C., their hopes of God working *through the current historical processes* had become very dim. They had not experienced themselves as a self-governing people for four hundred years. No wonder they felt pessimistic about their nationalistic hopes via normal political processes!

As this pessimism deepened, the people gave up hope for their "present world" and started thinking that Israel's hope would not arrive until "the coming age" had come. This then became the source of their language between "this present age" and the "coming age" of the Messiah. This lead them to believe that such would only arise *via a cataclysmic event* which would bring the present age to an abrupt end and dramatically usher in the new age.

In this way apocalypticism arose as their kind of dream literature that reflected this dichotomous thinking (i.e. total negative present age view, total positive coming age view). Describing these ideas and expectations, apocalyptic literature became marked by the following distinct characteristics.

(1) Highly visual. You will find all apocalyptic literature as dominated by visions and visual images. It evokes all kinds of visual images on the theater of the mind. You will find this pattern in the biblical texts of *Daniel, Ezekiel, Zechariah,* and *Isaiah*. The same holds true for the extra-biblical books: *Baruch, IV Esdras, Assumption of Moses, Enoch* and the *Similitudes of Enoch*.

Visions and dreams comprise the central technology in apocalypticism. Beasley-Murray (1974) wrote, "John's visions of the end are those of an impressionist artist rather than the pictures of a photographer. For the most part they defy precision in application" (p. 23). This, by the way, makes them high "hypnotic" in nature (more about that later).

(2) Strange and weird. Though the authors wrote apocalyptic literature in prose (in contrast to OT prophecy which they wrote primarily as poetry), apocalypticism featured lots of weird symbolism: bizarre animals with multiple heads, horns, feet, toes, and eyes, demons and angels, etc. The apocalyptic did not represent the normal. It portrayed weird and unusual phenomenon which we usually associate with *an altered state of consciousness*. Think "exaggerated Stephen Spielberg film" and you'll get the essential idea of apocalyptism!

Robert D. Brinsmead (1981) wrote, "We could even say that apocalyptists resort to *a kind of religious cartooning*. This is not only a literary device for arresting attention, but it is an effective way to represent the transcendent things of the age to come."

No wonder people seldom fall asleep due to boredom in response to the apocalyptic (they may fall asleep into a trance-like state due to confusion, but not out of boredom!). The apocalyptic creates descriptions most vivid, colorful, and impressionistic. And if you have much familiarity with the way the Hebrew prophets wrote with all of their colorful imagery and exaggerated statements (Amos 1:2, Micah 1:4, Joel 3:18, Isa 51:9-23), you know that wildness and vividness of expression existed as simply part of the Hebraic perspective. The apocalyptists just went further. They gave full vent to their fertile imaginations as they painted extravagant and exotic pictures of the end of this aeon and the coming of the new one. Expect to get jolted when you read it.

(3) **Dualistic**. You can detect the strongly dualistic tendency by the way apocalyptism packaged its drama as a struggle between good and evil, light and darkness, and this age and the age to come, etc. Consequently, this black-or-white, either-or perspective consequently generated a strong and stern tone. It conveyed a stern attitude. For them, the believers could allow themselves no trucking with compromise, tolerance, or speculativeness. To read such literature feels like you just walked in on a Sunday morning during a Fundamentalistic Baptist Revival!

Yet given the times, this approach and attitude seemed most appropriate. The apocalyptists spoke in a time when people needed a definitive clear-cut world-view. In those days, believers would not do themselves any good by holding tentative, speculative, open-minded, and unsure views. That kind of thinking would have worked as a liability in those days of persecution. In apocalyptic, we see the faithful in the heat of the battle. The time had come for decisive action and clear-cut decisions.

In the times between the testaments, Persian and Hellenistic ideas began permeating Hebrew consciousness through apocalypses. For the first time, Platonic ideas of the dualistic nature of man's personality crept into their writings (see *The Method and Message of Jewish Apocalyptic*, by D. S. Russell, p. 140).

(4) **Judgment Day**. The primary focus of apocalypses arose from the fact that *their authors saw no hope* for the present age. The apocalyptists looked forward to the cataclysmic inbreaking of

God's kingdom that would initiate a new world and change everything.

Robert D. Brinsmead (1981) wrote, "Apocalyptic breathes the spirit of imminence." Because the apocalyptists lived in troublous times, they wrote in days of adversity and conflict. This partly explains why they wrote in code. Their material presented a revolutionary view. Accordingly, they saw earthquakes, epidemics, bloody moons, falling stars, and other cosmic signs as the birthpangs of the new age (*The Apocalyptic Movement,* Walter Schmithals).

Apostolic apocalyptic similarly describe an imminent coming of the Lord to judge that current evil age. Peter warned apocalyptically, "The end of all things is at hand." He saw a judgment beginning "at God's house" that would bring an end to the Jewish age/world (I Pet. 4:7,12).

The judgment motifs throughout John's *Apocalypse* evoke reminders of God's judgment on Egypt, Sodom, and Babylon. John saw the days of grace ending and God blowing the trumpets to pour out the plagues of his wrath against the harlot Babylon who had become guilty of the blood of his prophets and saints (Rev. 18:24). This represents a pure apocalyptic perspective.

(5) Anti-establishmentarianism and inflammatory. One thing you can count on from the apocalyptists--they took a lot of interest in the destruction of their enemies. John pictured the martyrs crying out, "How long, O Lord, faithful and true, dost thou not judge?" In *The Pharisees,* R. T. Hereford wrote, "The apocalyptic literature is *Zealot literature.* It shows the inspiration, the ideas and religious and ethical conception of the Zealot movement ...The apocalyptic literature and the Zealot movement went hand in hand, the one providing the dangerous food and the other feasting on it and calling for more" (p. 124).

This also made apocalyptic *crisis literature.* Reflecting the same revolutionary sentiment, Paul wrote with an apocalyptic feel about the significance of the cross to his age.

> "To shame the wise, God has chosen what the world counts folly, and to shame what is strong, God has chosen what the

world counts weakness. He has chosen things low and contemptible, mere nothings, to overthrow the existing order" (I Cor. 1:27-28 NEB).

(6) Cultic Lifestyle. The Jewish apocalyptists tended to practice an esoteric and ascetic way of life. Some withdrew to the desert for a regimented piety. We see this most obviously in the apocalyptic community of Qumran which lived in the Dead Sea wilderness. Scholars have found sizable manuscripts of apocalyptic literature in the Dead Sea Scrolls, from the *"Commentaries"* to *"The War of the Sons of Light against the Sons of Darkness."*

(7) Prophetic. The apocalyptist represented a different kind of prophet. When you read the great Jewish prophets (Isaiah, Jeremiah, Elijah, etc.) you discover that they cried for justice in terms of political and social change. Not so the apocalyptists. What did they want? They wanted nothing less than *the dissolution of the world!* Apocalyptists pessimistically viewed history while optimistic viewing God's imminent inbreaking kingdom.

You can see such apocalyptism in the prophets (Isa. 24-27, 56-66, Ezek. 38-39, Zechariah, Joel 2 and 3, Daniel). D. S. Russell (1964) contends that the apocalyptists recast the prophetic hopes giving specific definition concerning "The Shape of Things to Come." They did not exist, he says, as bizarre plagiarists perverting the utterances of the prophets, but they consisted of men making a valuable and unique contribution to Jewish thought.

Ernest Kasemann went so far as to say,

"Apocalyptic was *the mother of all Christian theology* since we cannot really classify the preaching of Jesus as theology."

This explains *the apocalyptic events and words* that described the significance of the cross regarding the sun becoming dark, the earth quaking, the Temple's inner wall becoming torn apart, and the old world of sin, law, condemnation, and death ending. Obviously, then, the role of the apocalyptic in understanding the NT stands as immense.

APOCALYPTICISM
As An Altered State of Consciousness

What impression do you get from these general characteristics of apocalyptic literature? Do you come away with the feeling that apocalyptism stands as unique and bizarre? Good! It certainly functions as such. It also comprises the stuff of nightmares. This explains why those who fail to *index the information of Revelation* can literally "**hypnotize**" Christians and their children into all sorts of negative trances if they do not exercise care. The material and language of the apocalyptic, unless understood for what its nature, can create immense *millennial madness* (and as a psychologist I speak here from a psychological background).

Let me start with Brinsmead's reference of it as "religious cartooning;" that seems especially appropriate. Apocalyptic certainly engages in *caricature*. The way it draws ludicrous and grotesque portrayals of people, events, socio-political realities, etc. stands as highly similar to what today's political cartoonists can do with the faces, noses, eyes, tongues, lips, etc. of today's world leaders.

Imagine this wildness: a beast with 7-heads and 10-horns, the prevailing Lion of the tribe of Judah who looks like a slain Lamb and who has 7-horns and 7-eyes. These apocalyptic descriptions transcend logical thought and consistency, factual exactness, and static portrayals. Note also how these images tend to function in a manner that we might call kaleidoscopic. By this I mean that *as* you watch them (e.g. read the biblical text), *they keep changing*.

First there appears a Lion: powerful, majestic, impressive. The Lion of the tribe of Judah --an Israeli Lion, so bold, so brave, so appealing. Then the images begin shifting out as it transforms into ...a Lamb, a gentle, tender, soft, weak... and then it takes on the shape and indicates of having been slain. Now do you think that this represents mental TV at its best or what? (Rev. 5:1-14).

G. R. Beasley-Murray (1974) wrote,

> "The closest modern parallel to this mode of communication is the political cartoon, which has gained an established place in the popular press all over the world. The purpose of a cartoon is to

embody a message relating to the contemporary situation, whether it be of local, national, or international import... Frequently the situations depicted are deliberately exaggerated, and even made grotesque, in order that the message may be made plain..."

"It would be overpressing the parallel to suggest that the apocalyptists were religious cartoonists, for much of their writing is not in picture form. But it would not be misleading to compare their work with writings frequently illustrated by drawings, and at times containing whole chapters of strip cartoon. The book of Revelation uses the cartoon method more consistently than any other work of this order" (p. 16-17).

Political cartooning today offers a comparable counterpart to apocalyptic language. Imagine this one. See Bill Clinton's face on a gigantic fat man riding atop a horse labeled "The Economy." See the horse as so overwhelmed in size by the rider that the horse becomes flattened on the ground as its legs give way and go underneath him.

Do you need a blow by blow interpretation to understand that cartoon? Does not the cartoon immediately make its point? So with the apocalyptic images. To the recipients--the authors did not need to expound on the referents. The images did not so function. Nor did the images come primarily to provide intellectual information. They came to make emotional points and rhetorical points.

Apocalyptic language works in this way. This further explains why *a wooden literalness with apocalyptism cannot do it justice*. With wooden literalness you can't get past the image of the Son of Man speaking with a sword in his mouth (Rev. 1:12-20)! Listen to that one in your mind. Should we interpret that to mean that he spoke with garbled words? Lighten up! It represents *poetry*. Think of it as poetry taken to the nth-degree. It functions as an apocalyptic show to entertain you, to bless you, to encourage you, to shift your state (Rev. 1:1-3).

Apocalyptic primarily *aims to impact people emotionally*. It aims at the emotions, not the intellect. This explains why strict left-brain, literal intelligence serves so poorly as a tool for interpreting documents like *the Revelation of St. John*. Left-brain linear rationality will always fail to unlock its doors. The authors did not write such documents for human reason. They wrote such *to induce an invigorated, resilient emotional state*.

Many who have racked their brains over the texts have suffered vertigo (e.g. millennial madness!) trying to understand *Revelation*. They have created elaborate and ingenious (but ultimately stupid) charts. And they have all miss the point! By ignoring **the affective dimension**, they have treated such literature as if it comprised of propositional statements on eschatology. Wrong!

As an apocalyptist, John wrote his *Revelation* in order to move his readers *emotionally*. He sought to evoke in them a sense of assurance, feelings of joy in Christ's victory, a renewed sense of dedication, and courage to go on in the face of insurmountable odds. He wanted to "bless" them (Rev. 1:3). So, if you read *Revelation* and don't feel blessed--you can count on having misread and misinterpreted it. Count on that.

Now for apocalyptic to move you emotionally, you need to shift from left-brain processing to right-brain processing and you can do that by learning to *seek to get the big picture*. Jacques Ellul (1977) wrote, "I maintain that the Apocalypse must be read as a whole... The Apocalypse cannot be understood verse by verse" (p. 12).

The weird and strange nature of apocalyptic touches on another aspect of this literary style and one that over-serious Bible preachers usually miss. Namely, its **humor**. More often than not interprets completely spaced-out this facet of the work. Yet *humor* as those awarenesses "out of place in time or space without danger" provided one technology Jesus used a lot to shift consciousness and to create response potential. As a master at exaggeration, he used it to get his Pharisee listeners to lighten up, stop taking themselves so seriously, and see how that their over-seriousness did not make for a merry heart (Prov. 17:22).

The way John used the juxtaposition of strange and unexpected ideas, thoughts, images, metaphors, etc. in *Revelation* shows how he intended to create a cognitive jar within his readers. He used ideas and images because they do not fit. And this created *the apocalyptic humor*.

We see things as humorous when we recognize them as incongruous, exaggerated, jar usual expectations, etc. Cartoons and caricatures become humorous in this subtle way. We can even find satire, which functions by poking fun at important things and people, in apocalyptism (e.g. see the jeering and gloating over fallen Babylon, Rev. 18.).

So if you adopt an over-serious expository mind-set, it will work against you! If you approach *Revelation* in an attitude of dead seriousness, you will only predispose yourself against seeing its exaggeration and humor, and therefore its message.

Paul Minear (1981) wrote about the vision of the new city,

"The hyperbole reaches its highest point in the notation that each of the twelve gates had been carved out of a single pearl. The gates marked entrances through a wall measuring 144 cubits... What pearl can be this large? What gate this small? The hyperbole is so unimaginable as to be humorous, and yet a serious intent is hidden in the humor. How can one measure in spatial terms the point where a community encounters God's glory." (p. 138).

APOCALYPTIC THERAPY

In times of trouble, especially trouble that shakes up one's whole world, people need *emotional assurance* as much as if not more than rational explanations. In this way, apocalyptic literature offers more than propositional treatises, it offers new visions, new dreams, and new scenarios for the theater of the mind. When our world caves in, we need images big enough, wild enough, vigorous enough, memorable enough, and grand enough to capture our imagination, thrill our heart, excite our hopes, arouse us from lethargy, and *induce us into resourceful states*. And this functions as the design of NT apocalyptic literature.

Adela Yarbro Collins (1984) describes the language of *Revelation* as *expressive and evocative* in contrast to informational and cognitive language. "As expressive language, the book of Revelation creates *a virtual experience* for the hearer;" it elicits feelings (144). "The Apocalypse handles skillfully the hearers' thoughts, attitudes, and feelings by the use of effective symbols and a narrative plot that invites imaginative participation. This combination of effective symbols and artful plot is the key to the power of apocalyptic rhetoric" (145).

Without going into an extended discussion of the highly misunderstood phenomenon of "hypnosis" or how that some language operates by its very nature in an almost entirely hypnotic in way, this represents the power and danger of apocalyptic preaching and language. Such language induces the human nervous system into *virtual experience*. Now whether that experience functions as a healthy and holy one (seeing God's gift of love via the cross and resurrection of Christ in the mind's eye) or a hellish and unholy one (entertaining self-centered, narcissistic, ego-serving, or hateful, bitter ideas in the mind), such language operates powerfully to arouse emotions, induce moods, and install ideas in the mind. (See *Metamorphosis 14* #6, "Hypnosis: The Misunderstood Nature of Communication," Dec. 1994).

Why would the apocalyptists want to so arouse such emotions in their hearers? Answer: to facilitate *a catharsis*. What value would that serve? It would allow the recipients to articulate their negative feelings of anger and hostility, greed and resentment, envy and confusion, etc. Then via this expression, the recipients could release their built-up emotions. By this procedure old negative thoughts and emotions they might have stuffed inside in an unarticulated and vague form could become objectified and clarified (Eph. 4:26-27). Apocalyptic gives one an objective focus for purging one's emotions of confusion and anger.

As you use this perspective for viewing *Revelation*, you will find discover how this insight has usefully served (and continues to serve) believers. Sometimes the literature functions to *intensify* the emotions (whether fear and anger, disgust and impatience, or confidence and godly reverence). The apocalyptist has created vivid images that matched the fear already in his recipients (i.e. the beasts, the abyss of hell, the dragon, etc.). Locusts from hell and frog-like spirits from the mouth of the trinity of evil obviously evoke terror and dread. It attached such emotions to a corresponding image which later became released and transformed as the image became altered as we saw the symbols of evil defeat.

The apocalyptist created images that aroused the red-hot emotions of anger, rage, and fury. This functioned to develop a passionate desire that God would act to take vengeance on the anti-Christian forces (6:9-11, 2:16, 22-23). J.P.M. Sweet (1979) describes Chapters 13 to 18 of *Revelation* as "a paean of hate" designed to arouse those early believers from drifting into an unthinking conformity with the world. When you read these chapters aloud, its impact becomes "emotional as much as rational" (p. 13).

By using symbols rich in tradition which came loaded with emotions, the apocalyptist elicited and induced his readers into some very strong and powerful emotions. How did he portray his enemies? As Jezebels and Balaams! What world did they live in? Sodom and Egypt! What will God do to address the current evils? He will pour out the plagues of Egypt upon them. He will blow the trumpet of judgment upon their deeds. He will let loose the destroying locusts to torment them. Then, in the battle, when those enemies of heaven destroy his two witnesses, what will God do? He will cause them to rise again and ascend into heaven. That will vindicate them. No wonder this drama of John's *Apocalypse* carried such a powerful impact for those first-century Hebrew believers!

Without understanding every symbol or mystery in the book, you can experience a blessing via your reading. This becomes especially true since the author used rich, vivid, and profuse symbols to address more your emotions than your intellect. The very anonymity of the witnesses, as well as the lack of precision in pinpointing every referent, underscores *the language as primarily evocative and expressive,* rather than literal and informative.

How paradoxical that *"Revelation" does not reveal* all these mysteries! Most people find that it creates more mysteries and stimulates more curiosity than it satisfies. The Greek word, apocalypse, literally means "unveiling," and yet that which it unveils concerns not specific referents. What it unveils concerns *a renewed vision* of the person of Jesus. Thus, in that vision, we see Jesus as the New Covenant Messiah who made atonement for sin, who brought judgment on the old covenant universe (Judaism) and initiated "the new heavens and new earth" covenant world. By his parousia (presence or coming) the tree of life becomes available for all nations and peoples (Rev. 22:17).

The apocalypse vision stimulated several important emotions. It *evoked assurance*; he who superintends the candlesticks knows and walks in the midst of his new community. It evoked *reverential fear* of God; no beast from either sea or earth has any chance against him. It evoked *worshipful praise* for the prevailing Lamb slain from the foundation of the world. It evoked *motivation* to live in him, sealed by his blood, faithful and committed to his word.

John's original readers knew the dangers, powers, and threats before them. They did not need information about such. What did they need? They needed faith, hope, drive, inspiration, and motivation to hang-in, to endure, to keep believing right would prevail, that God would soon take control of things, that their enemies would not wipe them out, and that their faith would produce fruit. They needed to stay in an empowering state so they could stay Christianly resourceful.

Their latent, vague, and ambiguous feelings would become more explicit by the images in *Revelation*. This would enable them to handle their emotions more effectively in coping with that world-changing trauma. After all, what happens when anyone's world falls in? When one's vision of reality becomes painful? Usually, inappropriate thinking, feeling, and behaving. Some split with reality altogether and respond with schizophrenia, fantasy, unreality. Others escape into apathy, indifference, cynicism, and/or the deadening of their emotions, hopes, and beliefs. Others aggress in explosive and dangerous anger that shows up as destructiveness, belligerence, hatefulness, etc. (millennial madness!).

These represent the very kinds of problems believers faced as the great tribulation continued until that old universe fell. Some became apathetic and dead (Rev. 3:1-6, 3:14-16); others lost control and became explosive (13:10). Others became schizophrenic; they lived in delusions and lies (2:6,14,20-24).

Because many of the Hebrew believers did not cope well, John wrote the *Apocalypse* to provide *a spiritual technology* which would assist them in mastering the traumatic events with "power, love, and sound mind." Collins (1921) wrote,

> "The power of the Apocalypse lies in its ability to articulate this perceived crisis and to deal with it in an effective way" (p. 161).

Today we know that repressed anger in a powerless people can erupt in unpredictable ways. John did not counsel them to pretend, to merely think positively, to deny or rationalize. He wanted them to become angry at that which operated demonically in their world. Then they could transform that anger into effective action. Then they could crusade for justice out of their commitment as disciples (Rev. 14:4, 17:14).

Claude Levi-Strauss described apocalyptic literature as serving as *a form of therapy* (*Structural Anthropology*). The accumulative impact on one's mind and emotions by *Revelation's* fierce language, vivid pictures, traditional symbols, and liturgical context functions therapeutically. In this way, apocalypses function like the imprecatory Psalms.

The imprecatory *Psalms* refer to those raging psalms wherein the authors scream out in pain and confusion. Sometimes they cry out at God; sometimes at his enemies. Such imprecations (curses) function as a way to purge built-up emotions, to gain new vision, and to release tensions felt between present reality and hoped for visions of the future.

The One who made and knows us, knows how to bring healing to the soul. Accordingly, dramatically intense apocalypses come as a means for healing memories and empowering people. No wonder people have always turned to such literature when their world seems to have "gone to the devil."

As you read *Revelation* for the big emotional picture, open yourself up to the blessing of the text. Begin by thoroughly acquainting yourself with the OT scriptures. Baptize yourself in Hebrew mentality and terminology. Then the images and symbols will trigger in you a similar kind and quality of emotion which it probably evoked in them. I believe such reading will then empower you in new and surprising ways. It will induce resourceful states of mind (insight) and emotion (courage) when some dragon breathes down your neck.

INDEXING APOCALYPTIC REFERENTS

Given this brief background of apocalyptic literature, let's attempt to *index* what this literary device references in the book of *Revelation*. To what does John refer? Do the referents refer to something historical and in the past, or to something in the future? To what person, place, and event does (or will) his symbols refer?

Now since the first century, various authors have written literally thousands upon thousands of books on *Revelation*. Yet for all the research and interest, to date no system of interpretation exists without problems and difficulties. Some of this difficulty may exist because some of this information may comprise some of the "knowledge" that would "pass away" when the completion came (I Cor. 13:8).

Much of the difficulty with *Revelation*, however, lies in referencing the symbols of apocalyptic language itself. For instance, try your hand to apply the apocalyptic language of Psalm 18 to the life of David. We know the apocalyptic language of that Psalm refers to the past. Thoroughly study the life of David and then attempt to identify every apocalyptic symbol therein. Connect them with historical specifics. You will not succeed very well! What I think you might learn from that exercise, however, concerns *how David employed such language* for that trying time in his life and how apocalyptic language serves more of an emotional and evocative nature.

What does *Revelation* look like through the lens of the preterist view? Viewing the book as a picture of realized eschatology, it portrays how God judged and then brought to completion the last days of the Jewish theocracy at the destruction of Jerusalem in AD

70. This fits amazingly well the history of that age. In fact, to read the historical account of Josephus' *"The War of the Jews"* with the book of *Revelation* in the other hand creates an absolutely amazing synthesis and correlation. Try it.

Since contextually, *Revelation* specifically focuses on "things shortly to come" (1:1) it makes a lot of sense to read it as an oracle about "the end" of the old-covenant world of Judaism. If that concerns its primary reference, then its design primarily involved forewarning the believers and preparing them for getting through those hard times in a victorious way.

CONCLUSION

To talk intelligently about the NT passages which address "the end of the world" demands that we become informed and conversant with apocalyptic language. We have sought to do that in this chapter. Ignore the form and style of literature that Jesus and his apostles choose to package their "end of the world" statements in, and we first of all only manifest our own ignorance of the literary context of that day. Further, we will miss the rich symbolism of the Hebraic mind and fall prey to the danger of literalizing texts that the authors never meant for us to take literally. Consequently, that will head us in a direction that will leave us confused and disoriented regarding the referents of what those writers had in mind in using apocalyptic language.

We can now recognize apocalyptism as simply the *"wineskin"* that Jesus and his followers used to think and speak about the last days of that old covenant world. The *wine*, in this metaphor, consisted of the good-news of the new covenant age that broke into the world in that first century.

Chapter 8
**

INDEXING THE SIGNIFICANCE

*"What Significance Does The Ending
of Old Theocratic Israel Hold?"*

A great many things happened in AD 70. The events that then transpired dramatically affected Israel, the early Christian movement, Rome, the land, etc. The significance of those eschatological events had ramifications that extended not only to the world of history, but also to the world of spirit (i.e. covenant transition, completion, etc.). In Chapter Four I detailed many of the things concerning *the what* that happened. Now I want to specifically *index the significance or meaning* of those happenings.

IT BROUGHT A WORLD TO AN END
The World of Theocratic-Covenant Israel Ended

When you ask the question of the Hebrew mind, "What significance did the events of AD 70 hold for you?" you would receive hear, "**The world ended!**" When the Romans and Zealots destroyed the Jewish Temple *an eschatological event "of biblical proportions"(!) took place*. This explains why the Zealots stayed in the holy city to the very end. They sincerely believed, and expected, that God would miraculously save the day. They did not find it conceivable that God would forsake and abandon his Temple.

This concurs with Jesus' words about the dismantling of the Temple. His disciples equated such destruction with "the end of the world" (Matt. 24:1-3). And AD 70 came as a big "End" in terms of covenant history. After all, it brought to an end the Hebrew archives, priesthood, tribes, burnt offerings, Jerusalem as the nation's religious center, Israel as a theocracy (a theocratic nation), the old covenant (Judaism) as God's dispensation, the connection between Jew and Christian, etc.

Obviously, the Jewish people, or race, as such did not end in AD 70. As a people, they scattered abroad throughout the Roman Empire with many becoming members of the new covenant community and many forming groups of Reformed Judaism (AD 132). The world or universe that collapsed consisted of the world of the old covenant age (or aeon).

Prior to the crucifixion, Jesus predicted that the gigantic stones of the Temple would become dismantled stone by stone. A generation later, general-turned-historian, Josephus witnessed that event. He described the fire set by the Zealots in the Temple as melting the gold on the walls and furniture. As the gold melted it flowed down between the cracks in the stones. Later, the Roman soldiers retrieved the gold by dismantling the stones one by one.

Four mouths after the Jerusalem holocaust, Josephus marched with the Romans past Jerusalem on their way to Alexandria in Egypt, from where they went by ship to Rome. At that time, Josephus saw the ruined remains of Jerusalem and commented that unless one had seen the Temple standing there before--one would hardly believe that there had been anything on that site. After the Temple burned, General Titus decided to completely dismantle it in order to keep the fanatical Zealots from using it as a rallying point.

Contrast that history to the ongoing nonsense that you can read in countless magazines which continue to predict "the end of the world." Suddenly someone gets a revelation(!) that "we are living in the last days!" "We must now begin an 'end times countdown.'" So they use the "signs of the end" from Jesus' Olivet Apocalypse and *fail to index* those words in terms of what, when, where, and who. They erroneously conclude, "The Temple must become desecrated before the end comes, but the Temple no longer exists, so we must rebuild it so the new 'Romans' can destroy it!"

This illustrates the confusion and unsane logic that rises when one does not deal with *a text in context*. The *what* stands clear enough; the stones of the Temple at Jerusalem must become pulled down stone by stone. Yet they seem to ignore *the time element* ("before that generation passes away" Matt. 24:34-35). This results in people wanting to clear the Moslem Dome of the Rock and rebuild on the current Temple site. Why? So that Jerusalem can become besieged again by some new "Romans" which will then bring on the final war, so that the Temple can fall, so that the world can end, so that the new can come. How redundant! How unnecessary!

Do not these authors know about the eschatological events of AD 70? Surprisingly, *some do not*. Even more surprising are those who do know about it, and yet just dismissed it. "As shocking an event as this was [AD 70], it did not fulfill the prophecy concerning the abomination of desolation" (*The Chosen People*, Harold Stevener, p.4). "How did it not fulfill the prophecy?" Did Luke not substitute "Roman armies" for Matthew's more Hebraic phrase from Daniel, "abomination of desolation" (Luke 21:20)?

When the traumatic events of the great tribulation occurred during the 60s, many of the early messianic-Jews (Christians) wondered if the messianic age had begun with Christ. They began to wonder if Jesus truly existed as the Christ. They began to doubt the validity of their faith or whether things would get better. They felt so powerless against Imperial Rome and so inferior up against their more orthodox Hebrew brethren who treated them as apostates. As the hostility grew into outright persecution and ridicule, they felt sorely tempted to revert to their old-time religion. This served as the special kind of "apostasy" addressed in *Hebrews, Revelation,* and *II Peter*.

Now after the event, all of the post AD 70 documents recognize how "the world had ended." Nearly every piece of literature, among the Jews and Christians, referred to the Fall of Jerusalem and lamented it.

"They delivered... to the enemy the overthrown wall, and plundered the house, and burned the temple" (II Baruch 80.3). "And a Roman leader shall come to Syria, who shall burn down Solyma's (Jerusalem's) Temple with fire, and therewith slay many men, and shall waste the great land of the Jews with its broad way" (Sibylline Oracles 41:25-27). "Because they (the Jews) went to war, it (the Temple) was pulled down by their enemies" (Barnabas 16:4).

When the Roman destruction of Jerusalem brought an end to the Temple, priesthood, sacrifice, and genealogy it made (and continues to make) orthodox Mosaic Judaism impossible. The priesthood vanished, the cultus of sacrifice disappeared, etc. Then reformed Judaism, synagogue Judaism, and the Judaism of the scribes appeared.

The Jewish catastrophe of AD 70 meant the end of the Jewish nation as such. Brandon (1951) wrote,

"The Jews did, then, indeed receive a blow from which, as a nation, they never recovered. Although later, in the time of Hadrian, they rose once more in armed revolt against Rome, *their national existence had really terminated in A.D. 70*, for on the razed site of their Holy City a heathen soldiery now had its camp" (p. 166).

The destruction of the Temple became, and continues to serve as a major crisis for Judaism. Prior to that event, the Temple had always signified the Presence of God (the Shekinah of glory). It had always served as the place of the daily sacrifice (the cultus) and guaranteed Israel's place in election in God's plans. AD 70 changed all that.

Peter described *the ending of that world in cosmic and cataclysmic terms* in his second epistle (II Peter 3). Don K. Preston (1990) wrote an entire book about that chapter showing how it fulfilled "the predictions of the holy prophets and the commandment of the Lord and Savior." Therein he related its apocalyptic language to the thought and language patterns of the Hebrews especially about the "dissolving of the elements" with fire and the "earth" and "the works that are upon it" burning up. When people literalize such covenantal language and take it out of the context of the old covenant promises, they will inevitably fail to the author's original intent and message.

IT INITIATED THE TWO-STAGE END OF THE WORLD

We need to attain a crystal clarity about **what world ended** in AD 70. To what does, "the last days," have reference? Certainly not to the Christian age. After all, that age had just started. It referred to *the end of the Jewish age.* Check it out. In every case, the context for "the last days" always indicated the end of the Jewish age (Heb. 1:1). That comprised the age then coming to an end; God had marked it for completion.

Just how much importance should we give this? Much! The end of theocratic Judaism forever severed "the gospel of the grace of God" from the law so that the gospel could become truly and absolutely free from the womb that gave it birth. The world of Judaism depended on obedience to the Torah for right relationship with God. Yet the gospel had declared that ineffective. "By the works of law could no flesh be saved" (Rom. 3:20). Consequently, the law-process became a "dispensation of death" (II Cor. 3:6-9) which needed taken away.

Accordingly, *Jesus brought the law system to an end in two stages.* Stage one occurred with his first coming. In that coming, he personally fulfilled the law and accomplished for the race what we could not accomplish (Rom. 10:1-4, 8:1-4). In that advent, he became "our righteousness" (I Cor. 1:30). He finished the law's demands at the cross thus ending the animal sacrifice system of Judaism *in principle*. Stage two involved his second coming wherein he completed his gospel deliverance and brought judgment (the wrath of God) on those "wicked servants" thereby taking the kingdom from them and giving it to another nation (Matt. 21:43, 22:7).

"Where in the world do you come up with a two-stage deliverance? God has never delivered his people in that manner before!"

Oh really? It certainly fits *the prototype of Israel's two-stage deliverance from Egyptian captivity,* does it not? Stage one,

Moses took the children of Israel across the Red Sea to Mount Sinai (Exodus 14). There they entered covenant with God to become a theocratic nation (Exodus 19-20). Stage two, forty years later, Joshua brought the nation into the promised land for their inheritance (Joshua 1). Their deliverance did not occur suddenly, all at once, but *gradually* over the period of a generation.

Further, Jesus

"...has appeared once for all *at the end of the age* ['world' or Jewish dispensation] to put away sin by the sacrifice of himself. ...so, Christ will appear a second time, not to deal with sin but to save those who are eagerly waiting for him" (Hebrews 9:26-29).

The final saving at the parousia (his presence) would bring the kingdom in its completeness.

This accords with his words:

> "Look at the fig tree, and all the trees; as soon as they come out in leaf you see for yourselves and know that summer is already near. So also, when you see these things taking place, *you know that the kingdom of God is near.* Truly, I say to you, this generation will not pass away till all has taken place" (Luke 21:19-33).

Max King (1987) fittingly describes this two-stage eschaton as "the cross and the parousia of Christ" in his book by that title. He says that these "are in biblical eschatology what alpha and omega are in the Greek alphabet--the beginning and the end." In King's massive volume he wrote,

> "Christ's cross and parousia are the two foci of one complete, indivisible eschaton (end time) that pertain to the fulfillment of all redemptive history and prophecy within the closing period ('the last days') of the Old Testament aeon (age)" (ix).

Thus while the kingdom came in the old age (in the last days of that age), it did not immediately end it. There occurred *a time wherein the old and new ages overlapped* during which "the sons of the kingdom" interacted with "the sons of darkness" (Matt. 13:23-30, 36-43).

Finally, the old world ended with a great destruction as "the wrath of God" came upon them to the uttermost (I Thess. 2:14-16). Then, at that point in history, the entire old theocratic

Jewish world experienced an obliteration. The Roman-Jewish war wiped out its temple, priesthood, sacrifices, genealogies, city, land, etc. Its sun became dark, its moon no longer gave its light, its stars fell from heaven, and as "the powers of the heavens" it became shaken apart (Matt. 24:29).

Jesus had promised that some listening to him would not taste death until they saw "the kingdom of God come with power" (Matt. 16:27-28). Within that time-frame then, Jesus would also come "in the clouds of heaven" (a Hebraic phrase for God manifesting his power and majesty in a manifestation of judgment) and destroy the Temple. And that would end that age.

These verses lock in the time-frame for the fulfillment of biblical eschatology in a similar way that OT verses locked in the time-frame for the first coming of the Messiah. Yet as we well know, the scribes, Pharisees and Sadducees did not recognize the Messiah when he appeared. Why not? Because their *preconceived ideas* blinded them.

They had created certain expectations and ideas in their minds about the coming Messiah. They expected that he would come in a certain kingly manner and would kick the Romans out. Subsequently, when Jesus did not do those things, they did not recognize him as the king. He did not fit their expectations and beliefs! Nor did they expect the things that he did do. So while the messiah walked and talked in their presence, they did not "see" him. He had come to them, and they missed it. Expecting a political leader with a material kingdom blinded them to the spiritual reality.

Given this factual understanding regarding how key people missed his first coming, I here offer a hypothetical understanding at how so many good, sincere, and intelligent people have missed his second coming. *Suppose the same dynamic occurred with regard to his second coming?* After all, we also have the time frame for that event. But what if we do not see it today **because of our misconceptions** about its nature, manner, and result? What if, like the Pharisees, we also tend to *impose materialistic concepts* and literalistic hermeneutic on his return? What if our literal, material ideas about his coming has blinded us from seeing the spiritual truth of his second coming?

Indeed, *what if the eschaton judgment represented **a spiritual reality** rather than a literal one?* What if the destruction of sun, moon, and stars represented Hebraic apocalyptic language for a spiritual destruction? What if the resurrection, new heavens and earth, temple, light of the Son, marriage feast, etc. refer to spiritual values and reality, to the new covenant universe of the current Christian age, rather than something literal and material?

Biblical scholars have long taken cognizance of the time-element scriptures. They have no doubt that the early followers believed, received, and taught to look for Christ's return in their lifetime. If they erroneously believed such, what does that say about the validity of the rest of their words?

When Paul wrote his earliest epistles (*I & II Thessalonians*), the day of the Lord "is not near," nor at hand, it would not "soon" come (II Thess. 2:2-7). Signs and things had to first happen. And he could see such signs *already "at work"* (2:7), but not at hand. Yet a few years later, the end had become *"at hand"* (James 5:8, I Peter 4:7). Apostasy had started, Roman-Jew conflict had started, and unbelieving fleshly Israel behaved so as to "fill up the measure of their sins" for which they would receive God's wrath (I Thess. 2:14-16).

IT SAW THE OCCURRENCE OF THE "GREAT TRIBULATION"

Jesus warned that before the end there would arise a great tribulation. Concerning those apocalyptic times, Jesus warned,

> "Then shall be great tribulation, such as was not since the beginning of the world to this time, no, nor ever shall be. And except those days should be shortened, there should no flesh be saved..." (Matt. 24:21-22).

This occurred during the Roman-Jewish war which brought a holocaust on Israel between AD 66 and 72. This war claimed more than a million persons. Jerusalem suffered severe famine, inner corruption, civil war, and gruesome suffering during its siege.

During that time the Roman Army became the "abomination of desolation" i.e. the agent of God's judgment upon theocratic Israel. Her "armies" (Luke 21:20) functioned as the cause of the great destruction. In those years, they stood "in the holy place" (Matt. 24:15) which served as a sign to those who believed in Israel. At that sign, Jesus warned, his followers should flee to the mountains.

Did they? Did the Hebrew Christians flee prior to the great tribulation? Eusebius says many of them heeded the warning of Jesus when the abomination of desolation stood in the holy place. Tradition, following Eusebius, says that they fled *en masse* to Pella in AD 68 after the first siege and before the second one. Several traditions say that the Jerusalem Church stayed in Pella until the middle of the second century. Yet many scholars doubt this.

During this tribulation time the old creation groaned as it gave birth to the new order. Understanding this brings clarity to the significance of Romans 8 about the present time sufferings and about the empowering truths that enabled those believers to face those times with a resilient and bold attitude (Rom. 8:18-39).

This understanding offers both good-news and bad news. *The good news* for us? All of the passages about tribulation, rapture, etc. have long been fulfilled! They have reference to the past, not the future! Yet this serves as *bad news* for those who want some really juicy fear passages to whip up support, increase contributions, put "the fear of God" into people, hold people in suspense about the last days, and constantly offer sensational topics, etc. Too bad. (No more millennial madness! No more "Apocalypse Now!")

IT WITNESSED THE WRITINGS OF THE NT SCRIPTURES IN APOCALYPSES & TOUGH PASTORALS

To cope with the Zionistic madness that spread through Israel and to empower believers to deal with the end of the world, the apostles began a program for tightening down the hatch as they prepared them for the end. To detect this shift of emphasis in the apostolic writing, put *the Gospels* up against *the Pastoral epistles, Jude, II Peter, and/or Revelation and Hebrews*. Read a gospel, then read one of these other works.

Now step back. What immediately strikes your awareness? How does the spirit within these works offer something similar or something different? What states or moods do each of these pieces induce in you?

You will immediately notice *an immense difference* in the spirit of these pieces. The *Gospels* focus on good-news, the person of Jesus, etc. They present a spirit of openness and expansiveness. When you step into their atmosphere, you feel excited, hopeful, and bright.

Those later epistles, while still speaking about the good-news, focus more on *warnings about the coming tough times*. So they convey a different spirit. When you step into their atmosphere, you find a much more sober, serious, and urgent feel about them. Their spirit consists of one of alarm, conservatism, and defense. They plead for conformity, not creativity. They urge for a careful examination of people, not loving acceptance of all. The joyful excitement of the gospels gives way to a spirit of seriousness. Why? What explains this difference?

For years I noted these differences, wondered about them, but could not explain them. Each provided such *a different model for the Christian perspective* in terms of orientation, motivation, and spirit. Why? It only occurred to me *after* **indexing** *when* the authors wrote, the events occurring at that time in history, and the recipients to whom the authors wrote that I made the connection between how the events of the eschaton of AD 70 would have effected the later documents. That enabled me to make some important distinctions.

The reason for the conservative attitude and flavor in the Pastoral epistles, for the stringent exhortations, warnings of apostasy and severe judgment in "the day" that approached (*Hebrews*), the dichotomous black and white thinking) (*John's Epistles and Apocalypse*), and the get- tough message (*II Peter/Jude, the Timothy and Titus* Pastoral epistles) arose from the times. Such times tried the souls of believers. Such times severely challenged their faith. All these works arose during the 60s up against the background of Nero's insanity and the Zealots' madness.

In those tough times, the believers adapted a different strategy to survive. They had to *conserve* things. The time had come for the church to go underground. To cope with those end-time apocalyptic times, they had to become highly disciplined and serious. "The time was short," "the fashion of that world was passing away," "Satan would be crushed under the feet shortly" (Romans 13:11, 16:20, I Corinthians 7:26,29-31, 10:11).

The apostolic age came to a screeching halt in AD 70 when the two leading apostles (Peter and Paul) suffered martyred (AD 65). By AD 70, all of the others, even John, had died. The tradition of the aged John (the elder, not the apostle) in Ephesus goes against Jesus' prediction that John too would "taste of the cup" of martyrdom (Matthew 20:20-23).

Further, the Syriac "History of John" places his banishment under the time and persecution of Nero. Papias also recounts John's martyrdom as occurring at the hand of the Jews sometime before the last days of Jerusalem (*Revelation*, R. H. Charles). Clement (*Strom.* vii.17) states that the teachings of the apostles came to a close in the reign of Nero. Gregory of Nyssa put Peter, James, and John as martyrs between Stephen and Paul.

All this establishes the sixth decade as a critical time for the early Christians. It did not consist of a time for experimenting, developing their creativity, expressing tentativeness, exploring ecumenical concerns, etc. The time had come to shore things up and to stabilize the community with stringent administration rules and regulations. They would soon go underground. Does this not then explain the spirit, content, and atmosphere of the Pastorals? (And what does this say to us twenty centuries later if we build models of church organization based on those epistles?)

It explains why Paul urged the church at Ephesus to establish a "Religious Order of Widows" (I Tim. 5:3-16). He did not suggest this strictly for benevolence reasons, but to help those who had become "really widows." Why would there exist so many Jewish widows? Where would they come from? *The Roman/Jewish War!* Why would this be a problem in Ephesus? Because as Palestine would become devastated and emptied, the refugees would flee north to escape.

IT SAW THE "PERFECT" COME

Paul explained to the Corinthians some things about the coming end. "The time has grown very short...for the form of this world is passing away" (I Cor. 7:26-31). They then lived at the end of the ages (10:11). To face that transition, Paul wrote,

> "Love never ends; as for prophecies, they will pass away; as for tongues, they will cease; as for knowledge, it will pass away. For our knowledge is imperfect and our prophecy is imperfect; but *when the perfect comes, the imperfect will pass away*" (I Corinthians 13:8-10).

To what did this "perfect" or "complete" refer? The context indicates that "the complete" fulfills, and thereby makes unnecessary, certain prophecy, knowledge, and language--miraculous powers that communicated or validated the early Christian message. The context indicates that "the complete" makes the Christian community mature and grown up (I Cor. 13:11-12) in such a way that they no longer needed the miraculous supports. Now they could operate completely on "faith, hope, and love," which would enable people to see Jesus "face to face" (13:13).

What better fits the constraints of this description than *the new covenant in its completeness*? (Notice that I did not write "New Testament.") John similarly painted a portrait of the "new heaven and the new earth" as "the holy city, new Jerusalem," the bride of Christ *where people fully and completely experience the new covenant* (Rev. 21:1-8). Without doubt, during the interface of the transition period between the covenants, the old covenant only slowly began to faded out. Even then it "was growing old and ready to vanish away" ((Hebrews 8:13, AD 64).

Between the crucifixion (32) and the end of Jerusalem (70-72), God gave his old covenant people (theocratic Israel) *forty years of grace* to make the transition from the old to the new. With the coming of the new covenant in its fullness, it came as the holy bride and holy city of God coming down from heaven as "the new heavens and earth" (Revelation chs. 21-22). This brought the transitional period (between the cross and the parousia) to a close. This grace period allowed the transition from old covenant to new covenant to transpire, thereby giving the Israel of the flesh a chance to become the first to enter.

God allowed *this whole time period* (called "the last days," Gal. 4:4-6, Heb. 1:1, Acts 2:17) for the old to slowly pass away while simultaneously the new came into being more and more. These last days of the old covenant ended dramatically with a seven-year period of war and tribulation. It took three and a half years for the siege and overthrow of Jerusalem (7 and 31/2 represent special biblical numbers in the *Apocalypse*). Then came the last day (August 22) that ended the saga.

If this perspective of the new covenant movement serves as a new paradigm for you, put it to the test for yourself. Read through the NT books using this paradigm and see if it does not make more sense. (see Doug Adams' treatise entitled *"Transitional Christianity's Evolution."*)

The Hebrew writer explained the shift in the transitional period in AD 64.

> "In speaking of *a new covenant* [God] treats the first as obsolete. And what **is becoming** obsolete and growing old **is ready to vanish away**" (Heb. 8:13).

The author penned this just a few years prior to AD 70. Did you notice that this statement described the ending of a world *in the present tense?* The old covenant did not pass away all at once. It decayed. It slowly and gradually ebbed out. It *became* old. It transitioned out. Likewise, the new covenant came in steps and stages. So the completed system of the new covenant only slowly came.

This *transition period of forty years* stands as significant in biblical history. Forty days Moses spent on Mount Sinai, forty days the spies toured Canaan, and forty years Israel wandered the wilderness. The forty years signified the years of a generation became the time between the cross and the full inbreaking of the kingdom at the parousia of Christ. The old covenant only slowly passed away suddenly (it "became" old) by slowly decaying. Likewise, the new covenant came in stages: first to the Jews (Pentecost), then to the Samaritans (Acts 8), and finally to the Gentiles (Acts 10). During the transitional from one to the other, these two covenants interfaced.

Jerusalem's destruction not only coincided with the end of the Jewish State; it brought it about. Jesus spoke about it apocalyptically when he talked about the "sun" of that state becoming darkened, its "moon" turning to blood, and the "stars" of the theocracy falling into the seas (Matt. 24:29). These Hebraic and apocalyptic words only make sense when kept within the context of the ancient Hebrews' use of figures of speech. To literalize them and read into them ideas about the physical universe completely misunderstands the Bible's own terms. To do such commits *eisegesis* (reading into the text one's own ideas).

Did you grow up, as I did, with the perspective that the old dispensation completely ended at the cross? While I bought that idea, I had trouble with it for years. For if the old had ended, did not the *Temple* continue? Did not the *priests* continue to offer sacrifices for the next forty years? Did not the early Christians daily *attend the Temple* for worship (Acts 2-4)? Did not Paul go into the Temple to worship and even take a vow and cut his hair (Acts 21:17-26)? Did not James recommend it? Did not the *Hebrews* writer say in AD 66 that the old "*is* becoming obsolete and *is* growing old" (Hebrews 8:13)?

Truly, then the changing of the covenants occurred over a period of time. So while the new covenant began at the cross, God allowed the old law and covenant people forty years of grace to make the transition. That makes sense. After all, during the first ten years of the transition, *not one Gentile* became a part of the new covenant! Such did not occur until ten years after Pentecost, at Cornelius' house (Acts 10). Only then could the Gentiles actually participated in the "mystery of the gospel" (Eph. 3:5ff). It would take yet another five years before a mission to

Gentiles begin.

No wonder God had to plan for *a transition time* between the covenants. The old and new worlds co-existed and interfaced for a period of time. The gospel *"first* [went] to the Jews, *then* to the Gentiles" (Rom. 1:16-17). They had to preach the gospel to the whole world, then would come the end of the old age. Then those who stood there in the days of Jesus saw the coming of the new in all its glory and power (Matt. 16:27-28).

> "In speaking of a new covenant, he [God] treats the first as obsolete. And what *is becoming obsolete and growing old is ready to vanish away"* (Hebrews 8:13).

Look long and hard at that statement. This verse crucially indicates that as late as AD 64, the old covenant continued "becoming obsolete and growing old."

What began to pass away at the cross still existed in a way wherein it would "become obsolete" and "ready to vanish away" thirty-some years later. How could that exist if God had already completely ended it? Soon it would become completely taken away. "For yet a very little while, and the Coming One shall come and shall not tarry" (10:37). These verses make sense if we recognize that the kingdom came in its completeness in AD 70. "Let us be grateful for *receiving a kingdom* which cannot be shaken" (Hebrews 12:26-28).

In a similar way, God gave the world of Noah 120 years of grace (Gen. 6:3). During that time they could hear the word and respond. He gave the world of Judaism a transitional period of grace until the fullness of the Gentiles came in.

Just prior to his betrayal, Jesus left the temple and said, "Behold, your house is forsaken and desolate!" "All the righteous blood shed on the earth" (Palestine) would come upon that generation (Matt. 23:34-35,38). It would occur along with the dismantling of the Temple. Then he **time indexed** all of that to that current generation ("this generation will by no means pass away until all of these things take place" Matt. 24:34).

A similar transition period occurred when the "children of Israel" originally became theocratic Israel. God had planned (I assume) for them to take a couple months to leave Egypt and enter the Promise Land. But this depended on Israel responding in faith as true covenant people. Things went on schedule when they entered the wilderness at Sinai and received the covenant (Exodus 19-20). Then they went awry. They began complaining and rebelling. Eventually, the spies returned from Canaan with ten of them bringing back an "evil" report of bad faith in God (Numbers 13-14). So God declared, "You will never enter my rest" (Psalm 95:7, Heb. 3:11). He would not take them in with that attitude, so they "fell in the wilderness" (3:18). "The good word was not united in faith in the hearers" (4:2), so the two month interim period became a forty year interim (or transitional) period.

The *Hebrews* writer used this story (chs. 3-4) when he addressed the early Hebrew community. Why? Because they existed as that first generation that would shortly come to the end as Jesus predicted (Matt. 24:34-35). This forty year interim period between the old and new covenants (from the cross to the Jerusalem judgment) served as the critical redemptive time-frame.

Would history repeat itself? Would first-century Israel end their covenant-time as they had begun it? Would the unbelief of not listening to the message or integrating it in faith cause them also to "fall in the wilderness?"

The writer of *Hebrews* posed such as the question of the hour. Hear his exhortations: "While the promise of entering his rest remains, let us fear lest any of you be judged to have failed to reach it" (4:1). This does not have reference to ultimate salvation; the gift of eternal life functions as a gift. It does not work in a conditional "maybe you have it, maybe you don't" way. "There is no condemnation for those who are in Christ Jesus" (Romans 8:1). "The gift of God is eternal life through Jesus Christ our Lord" (Romans 6:23).

These believers stood on the verge of the completion of the new age (as "the perfect" increasing came, I Cor. 13:8-13). The old had become ready to vanish away (8:13), the "time of reformation" had come (9:10). That described "the rest" awaiting them--the ultimate "promise land," the "sabbath rest for the people of God" (4:9). "Let us therefore strive to enter that rest, that no one fall by the same sort of disobedience" (4:11).

Would they make the transition from the old world to the new world? Jesus had already spied out the new world by Jesus, the "pioneer" of their salvation (12:1-3). Would they get scared about the giants in the land? Would they see themselves as grasshoppers in their own eyes in comparison to the external features of the old covenant? Would they "go forth to him outside the camp" (13:13)? Would they look to "Jesus the pioneer and perfecter of our faith" (12:2)? They couldn't fool him. "Before him no creature is hidden, but all are open and laid bare to the eyes of him with whom we have to do" (4:13).

IT SAW THE RISE AND FALL OF ANTICHRIST

Something else happened during this time. *Nero torched Rome* and blamed the Christians. During the sixties, Nero's incipient insanity erupted. Historians now believe Emperor Nero had the fires set in Rome as part of his remodeling program.

In July 64 AD, the fire left Rome a charred mess. The fire set in Rome burned for ten days and leveled ten of its fourteen districts. To divert blame away from himself, Nero accused the Christians of incendiarism. This made them criminals to the state thereby allowing Nero to persecute them madly. At that time he let loose on the believers the most deliberately sadistic persecution. Nero had Christians sown up in the skins of wild animals upon whom he set loose savage hunting dogs. He had them enclosed in sacks with stones and flung into the Tiber River. He had them coated with pitch and set alight to light his palace gardens. Peter and Paul suffered martyrdom in 64 and 65 AD at the hands of that monster on Rome's throne.

Jesus referred to this in his Olivet Discourse (Matt. 24:1-35, Mark 13). He told about the end and the great tribulation in terms of the disciples being hauled into courts and tribunals, hated by all nations for his sake, betraying one another, etc. Many would fall away by following false prophets (e.g. Mt. 24:9-24, Lk. 21:10-19). During this tribulation, Nero exiled John to the island of Patmos and received his "revelation" (Revelation 1:9).

IT FULFILLED THE PAROUSIA OF JESUS' REVELATION

John's *Apocalypse* (which we call *"the book of Revelation"*) apocalyptically pictured the "last days" of the great Israeli Theocracy. This end of the old covenant held such fearful implications that John "saw" it and he fell back aghast in wonderment (Rev. 17:7).

But what did John not wonder about? The time element as to when it would occur. It would shortly occur.

> "The revelation of Jesus Christ, which God gave him to show to his servants what must soon take place...*the time is near*. ...These words are trustworthy and true ...to show his servants what *must soon take place*. And behold, *I am coming soon*. ...Do not seal up the words of the prophecy of this book, for *the time is near*. ...Behold *I am coming soon*.... Surely *I am coming soon.*" (Revelation 1:3, 22:6-7,10,12,20).

Those words do not allow for 2,000 years to pass before fulfillment. One would have to grossly distort the text to come up with that. If you apply its message to the fall of Jerusalem and the end of the theocracy, the cataclysmic events described here in apocalyptic terms fits very nicely. *Revelation* describes how the old covenant world of the Jewish theocracy came to an abrupt and cataclysmic end in AD 70 that changed everything.

Does this not also explain the importance of knowing the socio-political situation behind the AD 70 events? Knowing "the times" enable us to comprehend the "end of the world" statements and pictures. It facilitates our recognizing how the eschaton and the parousia occurred. Reading the verses apart from their context, and from the Hebraic mind-set with the Hebraic linguistic patterns, causes Westerns to over-literalize. And that causes a failure to see spiritually.

Who served as the beast from the sea? Nero and the entire imperial throne of Rome (Rev. 13:1-10). Who served as the lamb beast that seduced God's people to worship the Beast? The degenerate apostate Judaism which had become nationalistically militant. "The mark of the beast" referred to the social and religious persecution against the Christians under Nero, whose name just so happens, *in Hebrew*, to equate 666. "The fiery trial" arose from Nero's murderous rage in the 60's and ended with "the day of the Lord" that then stood "at hand" (I Peter 4:12-13,7).

IT WARNED THE CHURCH TO FLEE & SAW THE "RAPTURE"

To hear the radio and TV evangelists, you would think that the word "rapture" occurs hundreds of times in the Bible. Wrong! It occurs only one time! And, get this, most translations do not even use the word that passage!

> "We who are alive, who are left, shall be *caught up* together with them in the clouds to meet the Lord in the air; and so we shall always be with the Lord" (I Thess. 4:17).

I believe this refers to *the spiritual reality* that occurred when the old world ended, when God raised the dead by delivering them from Hades and bringing them into his presence, and then "catching up" the rest in the air (heavens) to complete the reality of the new covenant of sitting with Christ in heavenly places (Eph. 2:6).

Another kind of "rapture" occurred when the Jewish holocaust came. Evidence suggests that at least some of the Palestinian believers *escaped the great tribulation* by fleeing to Pella. This small town laid in the Decapolis beyond the Jordan river, north of Perea. King Herod Agrippa II opened the city to them as a safe asylum. Apparently, the Christian community stayed there until 126 AD when Rome permitted them to return. In 130 AD, Emperor of Rome, Hadrian, rebuilt Jerusalem calling it by a Latin name *Aelia Capitolina*.

Probably on the majority of the Hebrew Christians the events of AD 70 fell upon them disastrously. Many simple would not give up the old ways. So they failed to escape the destruction. The *Hebrews* writer addressed this problem in his epistle about "the Day" approaching which would bring a more severe judgment than what they would have received under Moses (Heb. 10:26-31).

These Palestinian Christians comprised Christendom's conservative branch in those early years. And the "sect of the Pharisees which believed" had come to dominate the central

Jerusalem Church. With this sect Paul got into trouble. They viewed his liberal ministry with a jaundiced eye and thought of him as a liberal to "the promises made to the fathers" (Acts 15:5). They demanded that he stop "preaching against Jerusalem and the temple" (Acts 21). Of course, in reality he did not preach "against" them. He simply announced the coming holocaust that would occur in that generation.

During the transitional period, this branch of the church remained thoroughly Jewish. They observed all of the Jewish ways even though Christian (circumcision, Temple worship, vows, kosher foods, etc. Acts 15:1). In AD 59, James, the leader of the Jerusalem Church, urged Paul to take a vow in the Temple because there existed tens of thousands of Jews who believed "and *they are all zealous of the law*" (Acts 21:20-21).

The thorough Jewishness of this Palestinian Christianity in heritage, thought, and practice explains how the book of *Hebrews* dealt with a problem quite foreign to us. The author spoke to Christians who seriously felt tempted to give up trusting faith in Jesus to return to the old covenant. The writer repeatedly affirmed that Jesus now stands *superior* as a priest of the *superior* covenant that brings *superior* promises.

Written against the backdrop of the Jewish War against Rome, *Hebrews* urges the Palestinian Christians to "go forth unto [Jesus] outside the camp, bearing abuse for him" (Heb. 13:13). They had to give up Judaism. The time had come. God would shortly bring in his unshakable kingdom in its completeness by means of a consuming fire to his adversaries (12:28-29).

AD 70 marks the Jewish (and to some extent Christian) holocaust that marked the final and complete rupture of the Christian Community from the Jewish Theocracy. Until AD 70, people found the Jewish and Christian communities indistinguishable in many respects (they *interfaced* that much!). Even Rome could not distinguish them. But after AD 70, that situation no longer existed. In AD 90 Judaism included a curse upon the Christians (the Birkat-ha-Minim) and recited it daily in its synagogue worship. After AD 70, Judaism cut off all connections with their brothers who "named the name of Jesus."

IT SAW THE REALIZATION
OF BIBLICAL ESCHATOLOGY

The *Hebrews* writer prepared the Christian community for the final "shaking of heaven and earth." The time of that final act of bringing in "the kingdom which could not be shaken" would come by the shaking down of the old kingdom so that the new could become completed (Heb. 12:25-29). Jesus predicted this. "So also, when you see these things taking place, you know that *the kingdom of God is near*. Truly, I say to you, this generation will not pass away till all has taken place" (Luke 21:31-32).

Futuristic theories about "the eschatological last days events" project these things into the future. In recent decades, they have popularized "tribulation," "rapture," "millennial," etc. Such theories make for sensational and hysterical preaching! Yet the most basic problem with such theories lies with their *failure to index time, place, context, people, etc.* Ignoring context, and failing to identify what those words meant to the original writers and recipients, creates fantastic fantasies.

With the fall of Jerusalem came the end of theocratic Israel. Accordingly, AD 70 pinpoints *when* the end came and *how* Jesus' promises about the end came to pass. The apocalyptic days occurred in the 60s of the first century. The *Hebrews* writer located the coming of the new covenant in its fullness, and the ending of the old, sometime after 64 (Hebrews 8:13). The perfect covenant came in its completeness in AD 70 which, accordingly, brought with it a whole new "millennium." Christ then reigned in a new way which he had not reigned before the fall of Jerusalem.

At that time, the "new heavens and earth" came. "*Heaven and earth,*" in Hebraic thought, referred to "authority and people," such as "the new authority (Jesus) and the new people" (the community of faith, the new children of Abraham). This "heavenly place" now contains no temple. Its temple consists of the Lord God the Almighty and the Lamb (Rev. 21:22). By the light of this new spiritual temple the nations walk and the kings of the earth bring their glory into it (Rev. 21:23).

With the fall of Jerusalem, the old and new covenants became finally and completely separated. Until then, the general populace recognized the young Christian movement primarily as a Jewish sect. Afterwards it stood on its own two feet and became thoroughly ecumenical. The church's pre-70 Hebraic nature gave way to a more ecumenical nature, one comprised of Hellenistic, Roman, African, and European influences. AD 70 liberated the Christian community from its cradle to go into all the world.

IT BROUGHT ABOUT "ETERNAL JUDGMENT"

In the context of speaking about "the end of the world," Jesus said the eschaton would find fulfilled in that generation (Matt. 24:34-35). To provide insight about when and how that would occur, Jesus listed specific signs. He also gave specific directions about what to do, namely, "flee to the mountains."

Simultaneously, while his auditors could identify the general time of *the last days* (plural) by watching for the signs, they would have no such signs for the specific *"last day"* (singular). No signs would signal that day. Jesus said that even he did not know the when of that specific day. And when that day came, no one could do anything at that time if they had not prepared themselves before it came (Matt. 24:36 through Matt. 25). On that day, no fleeing to the mountains would do any good. The time for action would have passed by. They would have no more days of grace. The judgment would then come upon them. That end would come as "a thief in the night." It would come like a thief to the unprepared, not to the prepared.

In AD 65, Peter said that judgment would begin at "the house of God" (the Jewish Theocracy/ Temple). God gave them forty-years of grace; then came the judgment. This judgment began at "the house of God" because the sins of the Jews had filled up God's patience and now his wrath coming upon them would come "to the uttermost" (I Thess. 2:16).

This accords with what Paul told the Thessalonians.

> "As to the times and the seasons, brethren, you have no need to have anything written to you. For you yourselves know well

that the day of the Lord will come like *a thief in the night.* When people say, 'There is peace and security,' [the Zionistic hope] then sudden destruction will come upon them as travail comes upon a woman with child, and there will be no escape. But *you* are not in darkness, brethren, for that day to surprise you like a thief..." (I Thess. 5:1-4).

The day would come like a thief. But *it would not come like a thief to those in the light!* Paul distinguished here what many fail to observe. Who would find themselves surprised by judgment? The unprepared. Those who prepared would **not** find themselves surprised. *The "thief in the night" coming* would only occur for the unprepared who heard, but did not learn how to prepare themselves.

Theologically, this preterist view sees all of the NT eschatology passages as fulfilled--fulfilled in AD 70. At that time Christ came for his own (I Thess. 4:13-18) and brought death and Hades to an end. At that time God called for the general resurrection of the dead into his eternal kingdom (John 5:28-29, I Cor. 15:1-59).

Realized covenant eschatology perceives the kingdom coming into the world over a period of time. Beginning with the baptizer's call for repentance, the inbreaking of the kingdom came with Jesus' preaching. God inaugurated the kingdom more fully on Pentecost but did not complete it until AD 70 when he removed all of the Old Covenant dimensions. Then he ushered in the "eternal kingdom" (II Peter 1:11).

IT SAW THE RESURRECTION OF THE DEAD

The text most people use to teach a "physical" resurrection of "the body" consists of the fifteenth chapter of I Corinthians. On many accounts all interpreters find this text challenging, intriguing, and not easily interpreted.

What first jumps out of the text when you begin reading it? Does not Paul first address some of the misconceptions and erroneous thinking prevalent among the Corinthians about the gospel? Yes, of course. They did not fully understand the very good-news of the grace of God.

One problem that immediately presents itself in this text involves indexing its context. Due to the fact that this document arises as a piece of correspondence, we do not have a direct statement about Paul's subject. Our orientation to this text puts us in a position like listening in to one side of a phone conversation. All we know involves the problem that some of the Corinthian believers had about the resurrection. Paul surfaced the problem. "How can some of you say that there is no resurrection of the dead?" (15:12).

Now on the surface this sounds as if they just didn't buy the concept of resurrection. *Not so.* They did! They very much believed in the resurrection of Jesus Christ. So what comprised their problem? Paul's response provides much that we find informative, yet it demands that one looks at it closely and think about it clearly. If you don't have your Bible out, get it; you'll need it.

Paul argued against their misunderstanding to put the lie to their false conclusions. Notice his convincing argument: "Christ has been raised from the dead"--you believe that, do you not (15:13)? "Those who have fallen asleep in Christ will rise from the dead"--you also believe that, do you not (15:18)? Yes, of course!

Now *if* these did not comprise powerful arguments *against* their misbeliefs, if they did not find these arguments persuasive, why would Paul use them? Obviously, he would not. If the Corinthians did not fully accept these arguments as legitimate reasonings, understandings and even *their current beliefs*, why would Paul use them? He would not. Conclusion? Paul felt those arguments would carry a lot of weight with them. If you don't think so, then you have Paul essentially reasoning in circles. "Why do you not believe in the resurrection of the dead because you already believe in the resurrection of the dead!"

Yet they found the statements convincing. Therefore if we examine them carefully, we can find out *what they did believe*, and deduce from that what they specifically mis-believed. First, they believed that Christ rose. Further, they already expected those sleeping in Christ to rise. Now we have at least two resurrections that they believed in.

What they did *not* believe in concerned the resurrection of *"the dead."* Who does this refer to? The non-Christian dead, e.g. *the Jewish dead*. That comprised the group that they did not believe would rise. Yet they had drawn a false conclusion. They had falsely concluded that anyone dead before Christ would not rise from the dead. Therefore Paul argued as he did. He asserted that the Christian dead comprised "the firstfruits" of the resurrection and that Christ would raise up the others, "each in his own order..." (15:23). "Then comes the end..."

What *"end"* does this refer to? Has this "end" ended? Or, will it yet end one of these days? Traditional beliefs, with which most of us grew up, push this "end" off into the far distant future. Yet in doing so we also put all of the other gospel blessings off into that future. Do you really feel prepared to do that? We create this misconception by *assuming* that "the end" he spoke about referred to the end of the material world and of the physical planet.

There exists a better way to think and conceptualize this "end." When you understand this other paradigm, it will provide you insight about Paul's statement and argument concerning the "baptism on behalf of the dead" (15:29).

To begin with, notice that this does not represent the first time Paul had brought up "the end" to the Corinthians. In discussing ancient Israel in the wilderness, he said that upon the Corinthians *"the end of the ages has come"* (10:11). He said the time had become short. So he wrote some *emergency orders* for those end-times.

> "I think that in view of the present distress..." (7:26).
> "Brethren, the appointed time has grown very short... For *the form of this world is passing away"* (7:29,31).

Paul fully expected himself and the Corinthians to live to see "the end." "Jesus Christ will sustain you to the end, guiltless in the day of our Lord Jesus Christ" (1:7-8). This comprises *the larger context* of his words to the Corinthians.

This contextualizes the statement, "then cometh the end..." so that it makes sense to think of it as referring to **the end of the Jewish age**. Elsewhere Paul spoke of the old covenant age as "an age of death" (II Cor. 3:3-18). In this passage, when the end comes, Jesus would deliver up the kingdom to his father. This would then fulfill and complete the redemptive enterprise.

One crystal clear thing about the passage concerns the last enemy--"death." What does this "death" refer to? Again, most *assume* "physical death." Yet the subject of the entire Bible, and particularly the gospel, concerns "spiritual death" which we defined as "separation from the life of God."

What then if the "death" under discussion here refers to spiritual death by which we experience resurrection through the gospel (I Cor. 15:1-4) and which the Law system of Judaism amplifies and makes worse? Did not Paul tell the Corinthians that the ministration of law consisted of *"the ministration of death"* (II Cor. 3:6-9)? Yes, he did.

Did not Paul write in this very chapter of I Corinthians 15 that *"the sting of death is sin and the power of sin is the law"* (15:56). Consider. **Why** Paul would bring up death, sin, and law at the end of I Corinthians 15? Could this refer to **the context** out of which Paul wrote this entire chapter all along? Yes. Perhaps the last enemy--of the old covenant--for the ending of that dispensation and the initiation of the new Christian world consisted of spiritual death that found it sting in sin which gained its power through law (15:56).

Would that not also explain how the Corinthians would find the victory and "judge the world" (6:2-3)? Christianity, *the spiritual system of grace through faith*, would soon conquer the old fleshly system of law through works. The last enemy to take out would consist of the Law System that gave sin its power.

But now, in that transitional time, two Israels existed side by side. One consisted of the child of promise (Isaac) and the other the child of the flesh (Ishmael). The child of promise owned his existence on grace through faith; the child of the flesh had his life based on law. One refers to the new covenant – Jerusalem which is above. The other to Mount Sinai and Hagar.

> "Now we, like Isaac, are children of promise. But as at that time he who was born according to the flesh persecuted him who was born according to the spirit, so it is now. But what does the

scripture say? 'Cast out the slave and her son; for the son of the slave shall not inherit with the son of the free woman.'" (Gal. 4:21-31).

This casting out of the old occurred in AD 70 with the destruction of the Temple, Jerusalem, and all of the key components of the old covenant system. Then God destroyed and defeated death, the last enemy, and put it under Christ's feet.

To further answer the confusions within the Corinthian church, Paul posed a couple of questions. These questions you have undoubtedly wondered about. "How are the dead raised? With what kind of body do they come?" (15:35).

Look again at Paul's responses. Notice that *Paul does not answer the "how" question*. He simply presupposes that the dead become raised by God's power. Paul addresses the "what kind of body" with which they come. What does he say about that?

In essence he first comments that the question does not compute. He categorizes the question as a dumb question. "You foolish man!" (15:36). The question itself lacks logic and sense. It lacks well-formedness. How does it lack reason? What about the question seems foolish?

The foolishness of the question arises from the fact that the "kind of body" stands as *completely different* from the kind of body planted in the ground. "What you sow does not come to life unless it dies"--degenerates, decays, decomposes, i.e. destroyed. The "bare kernel" that one plants dies and then comes forth with "a body that God has chosen" (15:38). Thus, "What you sow is *not* the body which is to be..."

Paul underscores the importance of this *different nature* in this next paragraph. "Not all flesh is alike... There are celestial bodies and there are terrestrial bodies" (15:39-41). Paul identifies some broad and extensive differences between the physical body and the spiritual body. Among his distinctions he includes the following:

Physical Body	**Spiritual Body**
Perishable	Imperishable
Dishonor	Glory
Weakness	Power

156

Physical	Spiritual
Living Being (soul)	Life-giving Spirit
Dust	Heaven
Image of man	Image of man of heaven
Flesh & blood	Kingdom

The "secret" about resurrection lies in the fact that it merely exists as *the means for entering the kingdom*. In this regard, two ways exist for one to enter into the kingdom: resurrection or transformation. Hence, "We shall not all sleep; but we shall all be changed" (15:51).

When does this occur? At the last trumpet. What would happen then? "The dead will be raised" and "we shall be changed." **The meaning of this?** *"Death is swallowed up in victory."* The Lord Jesus Christ has conquered the power of sin with its sting of death as empowered by Law and completely defeated it (15:54-58).

You now have two choices for constructing your understanding about *the time element for when* this "resurrection" would occur. **Choice one**: believe that the "end" under consideration concerns the end of "time" itself when the material planet comes to an end. **Choice two**: believe that the end concerned the end of the Jewish age/world, when Jesus "brought to light through the gospel" the "life and immortality" and fulfilled the new covenant (II Tim. 1:10).

If you opt for the first interpretation, then you have not yet put on immortality, you have not yet put on the spiritual body, you have not yet inherited the kingdom, you have not yet received the victory over sin and death (the last enemy). All these, and many other blessings, lie in the future. Today you wait for them. For you, victory has not yet swallowed up death. For you, the power of sin and the sting of death still operates because **Law** still empowers sin, so you "are under law" not grace (Rom. 6:14-15).

If you opt for the second interpretation, then you have put on immortality when you received the gospel. You thereby entered the kingdom. The kingdom (or reign of God) has come into your life. You now experience resurrection into the victory of Jesus. God has completely dealt with the "death" system ("the ministration of death" II Cor. 3:6-18) and put that last enemy under the foot of Jesus. You can triumphantly sing, "O death, where is thy victory?" "O death, where is thy sting?" (15:55).

The first interpretation treats this "resurrection" as resurrection into a new *material* "spiritual" body. The second interpretation treats the resurrection as something beyond "flesh and blood" (15:50), and having to do with our deeper and more internal real nature--and a current reality.

The first interpretation views this chapter in a literalistic and materialistic way. The second interpretation views it spiritually. Of course, neither interpretation changes the overall point of the message. The good-news remains the same as view through either perspective. But with the first, you posit all the gospel blessings *into the future* and must believe that the dead still go to Hades/Sheol to wait for some future redemptive act. With the second view you posit these empowering blessings as *now realized*--in the kingdom, something not entered by flesh and blood, but by the spirit.

CONCLUSION

Why did Jesus predicted the "end of the world" in his generation? Because the "sun" of the old covenant universe would soon darken, its "moon" would soon fail to give its light and its "stars" fall from the heavens. An age would soon come to its designated end. The last days had already started (I John 2:18) and the full commencement of the new stood at the door, ready to dawn upon the world. And, that all this did happen as predicted gives tremendous credibility to the Judeo-Christian world-view and the scriptures.

Edward Stevens, editor for the preterist journal, *Kingdom Counsel*, wrote an article in that publication detailing seventeen preterist principles and their implications for us today. He concluded with this statement, "Preterists are the only ones who can have a consistently optimistic worldview both now and for the indefinitely long future ahead." (Sept.-Oct., 1991 issue, p. 13,).

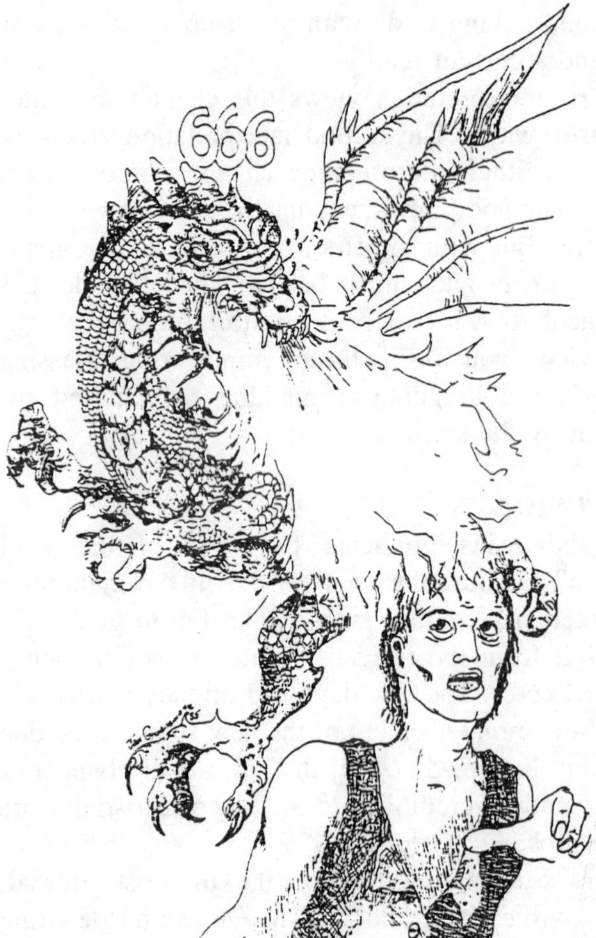
666

Chapter 9
**

INDEXING THE HOW

How Did the World End?

Opening the book of *Revelation* feels like sitting in the front row at a movie for "Jurassic Park! Suddenly, you find yourself in a very different terrain where strange and wild creatures come and go, where doors open to the heavens as well as to the pits of hell, where beasts and dragons, eagles and angels appear and vanish, and where all kinds of other strange and fantastic things occur. What does this vision mean? What does it refer to? To what do these things have reference?

In a word, *Revelation* reveals a vivid, terrifying, and apocalyptic description of *the end of the world*. More specifically it refers to how God ended the world of his old theocratic kingdom--Israel. *Revelation's* oracle of the end addressed the Hebrew believers prior to Jerusalem's fall which ended the world of ancient Israel.

We can think of *Revelation* as picking up the story where *Hebrews* left off. It shows *how* God fulfilled his promises to Israel about a kingly priest-Messiah. Accordingly, Jesus first appears in the midst of the Candelabra providing the true light for the temple as the mediating priest and the overseeing Lord (ch. 1).And from there he exercised his overseer powers to the churches to tell about the end of that old world and his coming to bring in "the new heavens and the new earth."

REVELATION'S DATE-LINE

Dominant in *Revelation* you will find the message of *the*

imminence of judgment. Judgment will happen "shortly" or "quickly." Judgment lies "at hand." The writer even pleads, "Lord Jesus, come" (1:1,3, 22:6-7,10, 12,18,20, 6:9-11). "The days are numbered" (9:4,11). "There was to be no more delay" (ch. 10:6). Question. Why don't fundamentalists (who say they want to take the book literally) take these statements literally? The author presents these statements as literal, direct, and propositional as any statements he makes.

And how different this stands when you compare it to the closing of Daniel's vision. The angel told Daniel to seal up his vision until the time for fulfillment, which in his case would not occur for another 500 years (Dan. 12:9). In contrast, the angel told John not to seal up his vision, "for the time is near" (Rev. 22:10). The message, "do not seal up the prophecy," came precisely because *Revelation's* content would shortly happen. Its fulfillment stood at hand (1:1,3, 22:6-17). The angel told Daniel, conversely, to seal up his prophecy because the fulfillment would not occur soon. Using this biblical contrast means that the angel thought 500 year stretched beyond the scope of "at hand."

In *Revelation*, we see *old Jerusalem* giving way to *the new heavenly Jerusalem* which stands open to all nations (21:26). The marriage of the bride (the church who has become the new Israel) now occurs (19:7ff, 21:1-4). Now the new covenant which began 40 years ago on Pentecost (AD 30) comes in its fulfillment (21:1-8).

If we accept the early-date, then John produced *Revelation* in the spring of 68, when Nero madly persecuted the Christians and when the Roman legions had laid siege on Jerusalem. With that background, this book's voice would have spoken in a dramatically relevant way to its readers, would it not? It would have powerfully spoken to the traumatic events then occurring. This would give profound significance to the repetitive time statements of the end as "at hand." All of this would nicely fit the socio-political times of the 60s.

Situationally, *Revelation* indicates pre-siege conditions in Jerusalem. It pictures the temple still standing (ch. 11) and Israel intact. If someone wrote the book twenty years later, there exists not the slightest indication that Jerusalem had already suffered total destruction. In *Early Days of Christianity*, F. W. Farrar wrote, "if the Temple was no longer standing in Jerusalem" at this writing, "then the language and sequel of that vision would be unreal and misleading." Scholar R. H. Charles dated Revelation 11 as pre-70.

Robinson (1976) linked Rev. 11, 17, and 18 with the events in Jerusalem and Rome.

> "The Apocalypse, unless the product of a perfervid and psychotic imagination, was written out of the intense experiences of the Christian suffering at the hands of the imperial authorities, represented by the 'beast at Babylon' (see 6:9-11, 17:6, 18:20,24, 19:2, 20:4)...if something quite traumatic had not already occurred in Rome which was psychologically still very vivid, the vindictive reaction, portraying a blood-bath of universal proportions (14:20), is scarcely credible. The sole question is what terrible events are here being evoked." (p. 230).

In terms of the book's date-line, *John's time key* suggests a time of writing during the period of the sixth king (17:10-12). The line of the Caesars began with Julius Caesar. After him came Augustus, Tiberius, Caligula, Claudius, **Nero**, Galba, Otho, Vitellius, Vespasian, Titus, Domitian. These Roman emperors derived their official title (Caesar) from Julius. "There can be no reason in fact or history to justify omitting Julius from the count of Caesars of Rome, and only the demands of a theory to provide a later date for Revelation has caused it to be done." (Wallace, *Revelation*, 371)

We supplement this argument with John's symbolic number, *the famous Beast number of 666*. John used this to designate "the number of the Beast." In Hebrew, this identifies "Nero Caesar" (13:16-18).

$$200 + 60 + 100 \quad 50 + 6 + 200 + 50 = 666$$

נְרוֹן קֵסַר

THE NEW COMPLETES THE OLD

Taking all of the Hebrew metaphors, John created word pictures that as much as said: "Let General Titus take the Jewish candelabra from the Temple of Solomon back to Rome as part of his spoil from the War--the True Light yet shines! Let the Roman Legions set fire to the Temple, burn it to the ground, throw down one stone upon another to recover the melted gold, and put the Roman Standards on mount that once God declared holy--for now we have a new covenant where no need exists for the earthly Temple. 'For its temple is the Lord God the Almighty and the Lamb'" (21:22). What power this would have conveyed in face of the siege and fall of Jerusalem!

Revelation details the concluding days of *the forty year transition period* between the cross and the parousia presence of Christ. Here the words that Jesus uttered as he walked out of the temple about that Temple ("your house was left to you desolate" Matt. 23:38) came true with a vengeance. Here *Revelation* finished "the mystery of God" that brought an end to the time of the Torah Covenant (10:7).

The idea within Jewish thought had so wedded the Messianic Age with the Temple, they could not think of Messianic age without temple. *Revelation's* **templeless Jerusalem** reflects the radical Christian idea of an internal temple. *Revelation* further totally repudiated the old external and earthly Jerusalem. In God's sight, had become no more than another "Sodom and Egypt" (Rev. 11:8). The new Jerusalem (i.e. church) would soon come down from heaven and replace the old as part of the new covenant.

This "holy city Jerusalem" coming "down out of heaven from God" comprises the new covenant of Christ's bride (21:10). This "beloved city" (20:8) now becomes the center of the kingdom for everlasting age of the new covenant. When the tail of the dragon had wiped out the former stars of heaven (12:4, 8:12), it made room for the new Jerusalem. This separated the messiah believers from those who had become "the synagogue of Satan" (3:9,12), i.e. Zionistic Israel with its national and racial hope.

The "perfect" had come (I Cor. 13:8-13)--the completion of

God's plan for man reached its designed end of people experiencing a whole new system of love and grace, of forgiveness and renewal. "Behold, I make all things new!" (Rev. 21:5). Now the water of life flows freely from the throne, without payment (21:6). Now holy Jerusalem appears in its completeness in the world (21:9ff). Now the water of life flows from the throne of God and of the Lamb "healing" for the nations (22:1-5). Now the lamp of the Lamb comprises the spiritual light (21:23).

THE OLD ENDS IN JUDGMENT

How did the kingdom of God come into the world? *Slowly and imperceptibly*. It slowly progressed in the same way that leaven slowly permeates bread or that seed slowly grows and matures in the ground (Matt. 13:24-30, 36-43, 31-33). The kingdom began in such an exceedingly small manner that many did not even perceive it.

The kingdom not only had insignificant beginnings, but came without observation.

> "The kingdom of God is not coming with signs to be observed ...for behold, the kingdom of God is in the midst of you" (Luke 17:20-21).

The growth parables reflected that the kingdom would come over a period of time. There would first exist a transitional period between the covenants. This gave the theocracy time to adjust to this change.

Eventually, the seeds Jesus *et al.* planted of the gospel of the kingdom reached maturity. The time had now come to separate tares from wheat; the day of judgment had drawn near. This identified the meaning of the AD 70 catastrophe which shifted the nature of the church from existing primarily as a Jewish phenomena. After the judgment of Judaism, Christianity became truly international and universal. Then, as the influence of the Jerusalem Hebrew church waned, all "nations" and "kings" began to come into the kingdom "bringing their glory into it" (Rev. 21:24).

Now God would blow his trumpets on the age of Judaism and pour out his "bowls of wrath" on those who had become

"Egyptians" to his new covenant people; those who had stored up transgressions. The cosmic catastrophe would consist of a total revolution in the spiritual world. The signs of this end (a darkened sun, a lurid moon, showers of meteors, shriveling heavens, and falling stars) Hebraically describe the socio-political crises (compare Isaiah 2:12,19, 13:10, 34:3-4, 50:3, 63:4, Jer. 4:23-26, Ezek. 32:7-8, Joel 2:10,31, 3:4,15, Hos. 10:8, Nah. 1:6, Mal. 3:2).

THE END CAME GALLOPING IN
VIA THE FOUR HORSES OF THE APOCALYPSE

By detailing the parousia ("coming presence") of Jesus, *Revelation* identifies how he came and "visited" both the old theocracy and the new covenant community. This comprised his "Day of Visitation" (I Pet. 2:12). He visited the Jewish nation in judgment as the four horseman came with Rome's devastation (war, blood, destruction, famine, and death).

This "visitation" on Palestine did not exist as the only "day of the Lord." To the seven churches of Asia Minor (representative of all the churches) Jesus threatened special "visitations" if they didn't become more responsive to him and repent (Rev. 2:5,11,16, 3:19). He would "come" and take away their Candlestick if they didn't cast out their apathy, paganism, and Judaism from their ranks.

The *Revelation* oracle provided warning for those who had "ears to hear" (a frequent refrain) so they could escape the socio-political-spiritual soon to occur judgment. God called upon them to leave Babylon (i.e. old Jerusalem) to avoid sharing in her plagues (18:4). If they would "keep" this message (by acting on the specific things mandated, 1:3, 22:7,9, 3:8), they would win the victory.

John wrote his *Revelation* to move them to hate evil, obey God, revere his word of judgment, endure afflictions, and follow the Lamb. The revelation provided them a clarifying vision of their Christian reality, majesty, and power, hence, "The revelation (revealing) of Jesus Christ... (1:1).

Actually, in God's patience, he had put off judgment for a very long time. The martyrs had long cried out, "O Sovereign Lord, holy and true, how long before thou wilt judge and avenge our blood on those who dwell on the earth?" (6:9-11). God responded by saying he would now shortly come to judge (6:12-17).

This means that, as strange as it may seem, *judgment* serves as the good-news in Revelation (14:6, the only passage in *Revelation* that uses the term "gospel")! How would judgment function as good-news? By judging Babylon, the believers could depart (18:4) and separate themselves from that which had become a corruption. This would rescue them from those forces which had adopted the spirit of the antichrists. This corresponded to Jesus' warning to flee when they see the abomination that causes desolation (the desolating Roman armies surrounding Jerusalem, Luke 21:20).

The judgment in *Revelation* occurs not on the believers; in responding to the loved of the gospel, they have become freed to become God's new anointed: kings and priests to him (1:5-6, 5:9-10). God had also *sealed* them against any exposure to judgment (7:1-8). Judgment made them victors from the great tribulation (7:13-14). "Here is a call for the endurance of the saints, those who keep the commandments of God and the faith of Jesus" (14:12).

FACING THE END
Apocalypse Comes As A Technology For Empowering People

With the end of the world shortly to occur, John penned his *Apocalypse* to induce his reader into some empowering states. "Blessed is he who reads aloud the words of the prophecy, and blessed are those who hear, and who keep what is written therein; for the time is near" (1:3). He wrote this encouragement literature not so someone could use it as "end of the world" sensationalism. John sought to induce *joyous confidence* in his readers. He had no intention of scaring the daylights out of them!

Though the imagery, at times, feels fearful, bizarre, and weird, and at other times comes across as full of contempt and revenge,

John always intended to empower his readers. Making intellectual sense of *Revelation* does not appear near as important as *getting the emotional point* (as mentioned earlier about the nature of apocalyptic language).

Though the content spoke about the imminent coming of Jesus, the end of a world, and the beginning of "the new heavens and the new earth," John did not write systematic theology. He rather created *an audio-visual drama* to have read aloud in a setting of worship to bring understanding (1:3). Experienced as an act of worship, it becomes evident that we should not seek to interpret its referents literally, but spiritually.

John's *Apocalypse* primarily addresses one's emotional state. This explains why we find its images difficult to discern while its motifs we can easily appreciate. He wrote, not with the logic and precise definitions of a scholar, but with the wild imagination of a visionary on a holy mission! The book does not provide photographs of the future. It rather unveiled the person of Jesus and showed how that Living One empowers people to face the future with courageous faith.

Try it on for yourself. Sit down and imagine you have a Hebrew heritage and live in the first century about AD 68, then read the book of *Revelation*. Read it all at one sitting. Notice how this reading effects you? What emotions does it evoke? Imagine now that you hear it read dramatically from the position of a sufferer in the first century wanting that old world to end. What states of consciousness would that induce in you? What resources would it access?

Experiencing *Revelation's* emotional impact necessitates putting yourself in the place of a first century recipient. Only then can you listen to it from that original recipient position. Then notice the feelings that well up within as you see the vivid drama unfold. Note how the repetition of the judgment scenes, the cycles of conflict, and the hymns of hallelujah induce various emotional states within.

For the Hebraically minded, *Revelation* will induce a powerful state of "power, love, and sound mind" (II Tim. 1:7). When handled apocalyptically, you will find it will empower one for effectively coping when one's world collapses around him. In this sense, *Revelation* functions essentially as *a handbook for coping* when times become utterly desperate.

Prior to the end of that world, the believers had fallen to complacency, compromise, and formalism (Chs 2 & 3). Sardis had died, but continued to put on a big show of being alive. Laodicea had become lukewarm, putrid, and nauseous. Ephesus kept busy with the niceties of church programs, although fallen from their first love. They defended the faith, but dissociated from their first-love. Pergamos and Thyatira went too far in accommodating to their culture; they compromised their faith and allowed Balaams and Jezebels to corrupt them.

All of these groups at some level continued to avoid reality. Instead of facing life using the resources of Christ, they took to escaping and pretending. This would not do them well in facing the great tribulation and end. They needed an apocalyptic vision of God's power, the new covenant's significance, and Christ's victory.

AN ORACLE AGAINST THEOCRATIC JUDAISM

In terms of content of *Revelation*, the book addressed the end of the old theocracy. This allowed the new "heavens and earth" to come in its fullness. Socio-politically, the problem the churches faced reflected *the early conflict with the Jews and the Judaizers* (2:6,9, 3:9, 11:13). This certainly indicates an early date. After 70, Judaism closed its ranks and took steps to exclude all "heretics" (meaning the Christians) from the synagogues.

John labeled these Judaizers by two OT allusions: *Balaamism or Nicolaitans* (the Greek word for Balaamites, 2:6,14) and *Jezebelism* (2:20). John pictures Jerusalem as "the harlot." She had become an unfaithful city, no longer holding good faith, but violating her marriage covenant (17:5, Isa. 1:21). Nor did this represent the first time. Jerusalem previously went into captivity to pagan Babylon and suffered there for 70 years. Now she had become "Babylon" (17:5, 11:8). (This designation, by the way, none of the other NT writers ever used with respect to Rome. Babylon arises from the Jewish biblical history of captivity to a pagan nation.)

Another Hebraic term John used provides a revealing insight. He called Israel those "of the earth" or "Palestinians." The "Land" or "Earth" came from a prophetic phrase for Israel in the prophets (note especially Isaiah 24:6 and 26:21 where the prophets use these terms for Israel and Jerusalem, e.g. Joel 1:2,14, 2:1, Jer. 6:12, 10:18, Hos. 4:1). These "inhabitants of the land," however, no longer comprised the faithful of Israel, but those fanatical Zealots who caused the demise of their nation.

The judgment would come upon *"the great city which is allegorically called Sodom and Egypt, where their Lord was crucified"* (11:8). Fleshly unbelieving Israel, who refused to make the covenantal shift, had become God's enemy (or "satan"). They "say they are Jews, but are not, but are of the synagogue of Satan" (2:9, 3:9). Jesus called upon these Judaizers to repent. If not, their unfaithful harlotry would make them a Babylon and they would suffer destruction. He called upon the believers among them to "come out from among her" (18:4).

As those of fleshly Israel rejected their messiah, God replaced them with *spiritual Israel*--those who demonstrate the faith of Abraham. They became his people, his 144,000 faithful ones. Consequently, the plagues that once fell on Egypt fall on the unbelievers. "He is not *a real Jew* who is one outwardly... He is a Jew who is one inwardly" (Rom. 2:29).

THE FINAL WORSHIP SERVICE
That Shifts to the New Covenant World

Something truly strange in the book of *Revelation*, and yet suggestively insightful, concerns the fact that *judgment day in this drama occurs in the context of worship*! Check it out. The liturgy motif not only dominates the book, it represents the main structure of the book (1:5-6, 4:8,11, 5:9-10, 7:10-12, 11:15,17-18, 12:10-12, 15:3-4, 19:1-10, 22:13).

Don't fret if you have difficulty seeing this. After all, you did not grow up in ancient Judaism. So no wonder you find its liturgical images as unfamiliar. That simply means you did not develop a familiarity with a Temple where the Shekinah of Glory resided, where priests slaughtered animal sacrifices on a great altar, where incense burned continually, where a Lampstand and a Table of Shewbread stood, or to which you would have gone for such holy convocations as Passover, Pentecost, Atonement, Tabernacles, or the Feast of Dedication.

Revelation feels alien, not because it deals with judgment, but because it represents *an entirely Hebraic mindset.* Its liturgy expresses a preeminently Jewish background and worship. It poignantly conveys truth packaged in ways appropriate to Jewish consciousness, namely, that the truth of Jesus Christ as the ultimate Pascal lamb. He alone, as the slain Lamb, stands worthy to open the sealed book of God's future (Ch. 5).

The oracle concerns the time when God would "measure the Temple" (11:1ff). Sweet takes this as a metaphor of divine protection and control. "The man whom Ezekiel saw (40:3ff), like John's angel at 21:15ff, measured the whole city. John measures the central shrine (naos) and altar, and those who worship there. Then the angel tells him to leave out the court outside. This, too, signifies people, not buildings. Even in Hebrew thought, the rabbis held that the true temple comprised the holy community.

Now "leave out" comes from the Greek word *ekbale* which means 'throw or send out.' So many scholars take the "naos" to represent the church, the true Israel (John 2:19f, Rev. 3:9) while that which lies outside refers to old Israel. This means that God would throw out the sons of the kingdom (Matt. 8:12), "a consequence of the destruction of Jerusalem in AD 70" (Revelation, 184).

In *Revelation,* "the mystery of God" as "announced to his servants the prophets" was about to become completed (10:7). What does that mystery consist of? *Mysterion* (in the NT) always concerns the secret purpose of God of uniting Jew and Gentile in one body by the cross (Eph. 3:3-6,9, Col. 1:26-27, 2:2, 4:3, Romans 15:26-27).

For ages, God hid this "mystery" within the holy scriptures of Judaism, but the Palestinian Zealots and the Hebrew Christians could not (and would not) accept the universality of the gospel. When the seventh angel sounded the seventh trumpet--this mystery became fulfilled. By reference, the historical fall of Jerusalem liberated Christianity from Judaism thereby allowing it to become a world-wide movement.

This worship lead to a clarifying vision of victory. It provided a new mental focus: Christians seeing themselves as loved, freed from sin, made kings and priests (1:5), Jesus as "alive for evermore" (1:17-19), conquering through him (2:7,11,17,28, 3:5,12,20-21), singing a new worship song (5:9-10), having a white robe (7:13-14), and complete assurance (11:15-19). Seeing that salvation, power, and the kingdom belong to God (12:10-11), that the Lamb will conquer (17:14, 19:6).

The new vision of God focused on his throne room (control center of the universe) and time beyond the present distresses (chs. 4-5, chs. 21-22). There stands the ever-living one who has the keys of death and Hades (1:17-19). Though current Jerusalem becomes a Sodom and Egypt, God has created a new Jerusalem (11:8, chs. 21-22).

CONCLUSION

You now know *what* world ended, *how* it ended, *when* it ended, *why* it ended, and *what* God accomplished by ending it. **To accurately understand *Revelation* necessitates indexing these facets of the book and its vision.** Otherwise, it becomes a text out of context which opens it up for distortion. Obviously, this short chapter, I have not and could not provide a verse by verse commentary of the fulfilled covenant eschatology viewpoint of the book of *Revelation*. I have rather focused on providing a gestalt portrayal of its overall meaning and design.

Chapter 10
**

CONSTRUCTING A VISION OF CHRISTIAN HOPE

Via Preterism

The preterist paradigm here presented expresses at its essence *a covenant view of salvation and eschatology*. With this paradigm it has viewed "the eschaton" as that period of covenant history between the cross and the fall of Jerusalem (roughly AD 30 to 70) when Jesus made his promised parousia (coming/ presence) into the world.

Via this paradigm, we perceive *God as having fulfilled* (or realized in the sense of "made real") ***all of the covenant promises God made to Abraham in the Christ event.*** This Christ event includes Jesus' incarnation, life, ministry, crucifixion, resurrection, and return in judgment. This entire "Christ event" transpired for the purpose of bringing an end to the old covenant economy of things (God relating to humanity through law) and initiating and completing the new covenant arrangement (God relating to through his grace manifested in his son).

This means that "the last things" (eschatos) of the Judaistic system have completely and totally reached their fulfillment and realization in Christ. What results from this? What does this mean? It means that *the everlasting new covenant era has begun and the perfect covenant has come*! We have now entered into the new age that the prophets foretold, namely, the age of the

Messiah, which the Bible calls "the everlasting age." This allows all men and women in all nations and cultures to experience the "kingdom of God." It has come; it now occurs; it exists within our minds-hearts (Luke 17:20-21).

Critics of this view often ask, "So what do we have yet to hope for?" "Doesn't this view undermine hope and faith?" In answering such questions I will take the ideas presented in the preterist paradigm and tie them together to create a representation of *the biblical vision of hope for the believer*.

The traditional hope says that Christ will one of these days literally return in the clouds to end the current Christian age (which scripture describes as "everlasting"!), to destroy the wicked, judge Israel, wipe out the Temple, resurrect the dead, reign supreme, etc. This view has wrong-headedly caused believers to assume the age of the Messiah has not yet "really" come. It has deceived many into thinking Christ he has not yet realized our hope, that our salvation stays in abeyance, that all the good things to come have not come, that he has put us "on hold"(!) until then.

I DON'T KNOW
IF I COULD THINK ABOUT IT THAT WAY

Well if you don't know if you could think about eschatology in terms of the preterist perception, then what would it take for you to accept *this perspective of the cross/parousia eschaton*? What shifts in your thinking and understanding would you have to make in order for you to adopt this view? To explore this question involves exploring the ideas, perspectives, and paradigms that you now hold, and operate from, and which currently forms your thinking.

If you began to adopt this paradigm, or even if you attempted to communicate it accurately to a friend (without misrepresenting it), what crucial presuppositions would you have to accept (or present)? Or, if you already believe and accept many of these understandings, then what underlying understandings would have to exist in order to buy into *the full realized eschatology* paradigm?

First, you would have to accept the importance of indexing any and every Bible context to what, when, where, who, how, why, etc.. The critical thinking hermeneutic tool of indexing **what** the Bible says about the "last things" (the details and content) would then become crucially important. Equally important would involve indexing **when** the text says those events will occur, to whom, where in what socio-political context, how, etc.

If you accept this *hermeneutic principle* of starting with the plain and propositional statements of a text rather than with the figurative and metaphorical statements, then I believe you will eventually index yourself into this paradigm (if you also aim for consistency). This factor lead me to this consistent preterist viewpoint.

For years, when I read the scriptures, I would open the Bible and begin reading *without* even questioning, "Who wrote this?" "When?" "To whom?" "About what?" I read the scriptures as if the authors had written it **me** in the Twentieth Century! Eventually, I recognized this as *an egotistic way* to study the Bible.

When you index the statements of the Bible and deal with Jesus' statement that "not one stone being left upon another" of the Temple when the "end of the world" comes, you realize that *this statement delimits those events* to a specific time frame. So does his statement, "This generation will not pass away until *all these things come to pass*" (Matt. 24:34). Beginning with these time statements and indexing "the last days" to the end of the then current Jewish theocracy covenant puts the statements into a specific time-context (Rev. 1:1, Heb. 1:2, Acts 2:17, I John 2:18, I Cor. 10:11).

Without doing such time-indexing, place-indexing, person-indexing, language-indexing, etc. of the biblical statements, you would end up engaging in the current fad of using **the ego-centric perspective** that *assumes* (wrongly so) that whatever the Bible says, it says to us and our generation. (Doesn't that border on the sin of arrogant pride?) A hermeneutic like that ignores context. And any text out of context inevitably becomes the basis for a pretext--for making it say whatever you want it to say. Haven't we had enough of that?

The egocentricity of always and unconditionally applying every text to yourself, to your generation, etc. assumes that you and your times exist as *the most important* dates in biblical history. It falsely assumes that the historical context of the apostolic age when Jesus introduced the new covenant into this world lacks much importance. It downplays the importance of the church as built upon the "foundation of the apostles and prophets, Jesus Christ being the chief corner stone" (Eph. 2:20-22).

In realized covenant eschatology, we take seriously the time statements as legitimate and inspired statements regarding **when** the writers specified the events would occur. Why do we not see these statements as "figurative?" Because we tend to use symbolism primarily when a subject becomes too complex, mysterious, abstract, and rich to describe in simple sensory-based language. This explains the Bible's often use of figurative language forms (literary devices, metaphors, etc.) to describe the "what" that will occur (especially Hebraic symbolism).

The subject of covenant fulfillment eschatology in the days of Christ and his apostles simply comprised a subject too rich and complex to describe without multilevel words. This does not, however, occur when they need to communicate *the "when" of time*. We and they alike can easily communicated the "when" of something. We do that by simply using time-language (temporal predicates: soon, long, short, now, coming, at hand, etc.). No problem in communicating **that!**

Second, to accept this view one has to esteem **covenant thinking** as very important for understanding the overall biblical story. This became another convincer for me. After all, the Bible essentially reveals the story of covenant. Read the Bible through from cover to cover. What kind of language will you find most predominant in it? Answer: *"story."* From Abraham, Noah, Moses, the children of Israel, the Judges, kingdoms, captivities to Assyria and Babylon, return from exile, to John, Jesus and the apostles, *covenant* and the covenant story comprises the most central motif throughout the Bible.

Accordingly, as you begin to **think covenantally**, you begin to think in terms of what God originally intended to do with his covenant-oath to Abraham. You begin to wonder how that related to and became moderated by the time of Torah to become ultimately fulfilled in Christ. Consider specifically the great covenant thinking in Galatians chapter three. This section offers an entire Bible overview from promise through law to the age of fulfillment in Christ (Gal. 3:6-28). *Thinking covenantally* becomes absolutely essential for anyone studying *Hebrews* and *Revelation*. Both documents indicate that the authors totally baptized their work in *Hebraic covenant thought* so that without understanding the covenant references, one **cannot** understand those "end time" books.

Thinking from the framework of covenant also facilitates your understanding about how to index the references of the text. If you open *Hebrews* and find, "in these last days," you know that it must indicate the last days of the old covenant. So with "hold your confidence firm to the end" (3:6,14). So with "as you see the day approaching" (10:25).

Third, to accept this view one needs to value the importance of distinguishing old and new covenants. Do you currently know how the old and new covenants differ? What specifically can you identify in the old covenant that made it weak, ineffective, and problematic (Romans 7) so that God "found fault" with it and promised a "new" covenant (Hebrews 8)?

As the first consisted of a material, physical, external, and literal covenant. That covenant focused on things physical and material. Based on law, it operated with a law orientation, hence conditional ("if you obey....then..."). "It made nothing perfect." Also, it could only identify the problem, it could not bring resolution, reconciliation, or a state of no-condemnation.

In contrast, we read that the second and new covenant operated as a *spiritual* covenant, one "not made with hands," not entered by "flesh and blood," and therefore "within you." It brought in a better hope by which God makes people "perfect" in relation to him, totally forgiven, under no condemnation, totally loved and secured. This makes the new covenant, grace-based and grace-oriented. It offers one a perfect standing before God and the power to live resourcefully.

The Pharisees could not see the messiah in their midst, or the kingdom of which he spoke. Why? Because they looked for a physical, political, material kingdom (Luke 17:20-21). Does this not continue as the problem for those who today have become "Christian in name, but Jew in spirit?" They think like old covenant people --focusing on a material temple or sanctuary, a special priesthood (ministers), external rituals, an external law (church creed), etc.

This, in my opinion, represents that which exists as fundamentally wrong with most organized Christian religion. We have not allowed the apostolic distinctions between the covenants to completely determine our understanding of the new. We have brought over too much of the old into the new thus contaminating it with old covenant law, legalism, work-righteousness, elitism, etc. We have become Christian in name, while maintaining old Zionist attitudes of superiority over others.

Accordingly, many "Christian" churches look, sound, and feel more Jewish in spirit than Christian. Many still emphasize a physical temple where people "go to the sanctuary" rather than *being* the sanctuary (I Cor. 3:16-17, 6:19-20). The emphasis lies upon passively experiencing "worship" happening to them, rather than their very life-style being the spiritual worship they offer to God (Romans 12:1-2). Communicants forget that they have become "a kingdom of priests" unto God, and no longer dependently need some priest (pastor) to represent them before God (I Peter 2:5,9).

Conversely, those who have truly caught *the spirit of the new covenant* realize that the torah has now become written on the heart, that the sanctuary of God exists in our heart, that we all exist as "kings and priests unto God," a holy nation, etc. (I Pet. 2:5,9, I Cor. 3:10-16, II Cor. 3). To say that the new covenant has become "spiritual" does not undermine its reality; it only asserts it as something **not** material and physical (Rom. 14:17). It has become something internal.

This identifies the area where preachers have done the most damage with the traditional view of eschatology. As people still think that the new yet remains to come in its fullness, and so keep waiting for the world to end, they live as essentially blinded to the presence of the kingdom now, to the power of the king now, and all the blessings currently available in this new age covenant. They want the "perfect" to come so that they can enter the age of the messiah, not realizing all of the messianic age blessings currently available. Consequently, many live impoverished and disempowered lives. They live fearfully, rather than with the spirit of "power, love, and sound mind" (II Tim. 1:7).

Now suppose, just for a moment, that the preterist viewpoint turns out **right on target**. Suppose, for the sake of argument, that Jesus has already returned in judgment on Israel and has already brought the world to an end, and has already initiated the completeness of the new world. Just pretend. Suppose that "the new heavens and the new earth" have come in its fullness --*spiritually* (rather than physically), and that believers now have all the messianic age blessings. Just imagine it.

Now **if** this represents the truth, wouldn't it then stand as really pathetic and sad to observe how defeated, fearful, paranoid, judgmental, passive, and disempowered so many Christians live their lives?! Like the Jews of the first century living in the presence of the Christ *and not seeing it*, these also would actually live in the presence of the kingdom, and also not see it, nor realize it. It happened once--in the first century when Jesus came. Could history have repeated itself in this respect?

Yet the new covenant initiated the grace of a greater era. Scripture says Jesus was "born under the law to redeem them that were under the law" (Gal. 4:4-6). Accordingly, when he came **he spiritualized the law**. Read the famous sermon on the mount. There *he spiritualized the true meaning of the Torah* (Matt. 5-7). The *Hebrews* writer said that in Christ, the temple, priesthood, sacrifices, incense, etc. have all become all spiritualized and realized. In fact, those external, physical, and material things actually existed as but "shadows" (shadowy images) of the reality (substance) in Christ (Hebrews 8-10).

So to live today, in this age of the messiah, thinking that the old still exists and that that old covenant dispensation has not fully ended, and that we do not have access to all of the messianic age blessings would describe a *blindness to reality*. Could this explain why Paul urged his first century readers to "**wake up to reality?**" "I think you have realized, the present time (AD 59) is of the highest importance--it is time to wake up to reality. Every day brings God's salvation nearer. The night [old covenant era] is nearly over, the day [new covenant age] has almost dawned." (Romans 13:11-12 Phillips).

Now if you begin with just these three basic presuppositions about...

- *How to treat the biblical text* (indexing its statements for time, place, person, process, etc.)
- *Thinking covenantally in perceiving the gospel of the grace of God* as essentially different and transcending the external old covenant of law,
- *As something that fulfills all of the literal and external facets of the old covenant* for something spiritual and non-material, then you will find the paradigm of realized covenant eschatology meaningful and fitting.

THE PRETERIST CHRISTIAN VISION OF HOPE

As a preterist, I believe that Jesus as the messiah has faithfully fulfilled his promises to bring an end to the world that he entered and that he did it in that generation as he predicted (Matt. 24:1-34). I believe that he faithfully fulfilled bringing judgment on that generation to the uttermost (Matt. 23:34-36, I Thess. 2:13-16). I believe that he faithfully brought in his kingdom with power and glory and then truly and initiated the new Christian age in its fullness (Mark 9:1). I believe he faithfully fulfilled his promises to "rapture" his church out of that tribulation, and to resurrect all those that slept in him. Accordingly, I believe that eternity has begun when the new covenant came in its fullness in AD 70. Therefore the everlasting age of the Messiah came as he promised.

The Christian vision of hope for me now means that we *have* eternal life (I John 5:11-12). We have "passed from death into life" (John 5:24). We now have a tabernacle made without hands, eternal in the heavens and that all of the blessings of the new covenant have become available to us in the here-and-now so that *we can begin to live the real-ized life of the kingdom* (Rev. 21-22).

This vision means that when we die, we have no need to go to a waiting place (Hades/Sheol). Nor do we have any need to go to judgment to determine if we made it or not(!). After all, God has already determined that in the Christ-event (Romans 5:1ff, 8:1ff). Recognizing that we have already died (spiritually in Christ), that we have already experienced burial (in water as a symbol), and have already experience resurrection in like manner as Christ (Romans 6:3-5 the symbolism of baptism), upon death we pass immediately and directly into the presence of God. What more could we ask for? What more could we anticipate and hope for?

Since "the perfect" has come with the completion of the new covenant the Christian vision of hope asserts that the old covenant saints have also now experience their redemption (Heb. 11:39-40). All who died in Jesus before AD 70 have also put on immortality and passed into the presence of God (I Cor 15). They do not wait in Hades for a resurrection and judgment. Since the parousia of Christ in AD 70, they have entered eternity and do rest from their labors.

This Christian vision of hope triumphantly says that Jesus has absolutely conquered the final enemy, spiritual death. Jesus has brought "life and immortality" to light through the gospel (II Tim. 1:10). Now when we die he immediately ushers us into eternity into his presence --because transformation has already occurred. We already have our "spiritual body."

LEARNING TO SEE
"THE NEW EARTH AND THE NEW HEAVENS"

> "Then I saw a new heaven and a new earth...I saw the holy city, new Jerusalem, coming down out of heaven from God, prepared as a bride adorned for her husband..." (Rev. 21:1-2).

Do you believe that the assembled-people of believers (the "church") exists today as the bride of Christ? Do you believe that she has married Christ? Have we experienced resurrection in order to marry another, even to him who rose from the dead or not (Romans 7:1-6)? My vision says we have. I believe it has happened--that the bride has come down as the new holy Jerusalem. I believe that explains why the old Jerusalem went through judgment.

> "I heard a loud voice from the throne saying, *'Behold, the dwelling of God is with men.* He will dwell with them, and they shall be his people, and God himself will be with them..." (Rev. 21:3).

This describes part of the preterist vision of hope today. God now "dwells with us." He lives within us so that our very being (or personality) has become his dwelling place (I Cor. 3:16-17, 6:19-20). Do you believe that? Or will that come to pass--one of these days?

More of *today's vision of hope*: "He will wipe away every tear from their eyes, and death shall be no more, neither shall there be mourning nor crying nor pain any more, for the former things have passed away" (Rev. 21:4). The "former things have passed away" or in Paul's words, "the old has passed away, behold, the new has come" (II Cor. 5:17). Paul identifies this as spiritual--"we regard no one from a human point of view" (II Cor. 5:16), "for we walk by faith, not by sight" (II Cor. 5:7).

What tears has he wiped away in this passage? The tears of sin, guilt, condemnation, rejection, damnation. No more mourning over that! No crying over that in this age! Why? Because the former things (old covenant of law) has passed away. We have an entirely new and different arrangement with God that includes total and ongoing forgiveness!

More hope real-ized:
> "He who sat upon the throne said, *'Behold, I made all things new!"* ...he said to me, 'It is done! I am the Alpha and the Omega, the beginning and the end. To the thirsty I will give from *the fountain of the water of life* without payment [there's grace!]. He who conquers shall have this heritage, and I will be his God and *he shall be my son."* (Rev. 21:5-8).

This new covenant vision sees the fountain of life as current reality--not as a future one.

For years I had trouble with these verses because they sounded so much like other NT passages about the new covenant age. Yet if these exist as the promises and hope of the messianic age at the end of the world, how does this differ from the Christian new covenant age? I couldn't answer such questions then. Now I know that the coming messianic age exists as the new covenant age brought in fully in AD 70.

More vision as another angel said,
> "'Come, I will show you *the Bride*, the wife of the Lamb.' And in the Spirit he carried me away to *a great, high mountain,* and showed me *the holy city Jerusalem* coming down out of heaven from God, having the glory of God, its radiance like a most rare jewel... it had a great, high wall, with twelve gates, and at the gates twelve angels, and on the gates the names of the twelve tribes of the sons of Israel were inscribed... the wall of the city had twelve foundations, and on them the twelve names of the twelve apostles of the Lamb." (Rev. 21:9-14).

What bride (or wife) of the Lamb comes in this vision? The church! The holy new Jerusalem as the new Israel (Romans 2:28-29, Gal. 6:16) built upon the foundation of the apostles. What a picture of the new covenant community! The fulfillment of those "children of Abraham" who by faith trust the messiah (Gal. 3:26-29).

The glory (brilliance, brightness, majesty) of this new creation consists of precious materials (Rev. 21:15-21). "The city was pure gold, clear as glass." And its size--a gigantic four-square sanctuary replicating Solomon's glorious inner sanctum.

> "I saw *no temple* in the city, for its temple is the Lord God the Almighty and the Lamb. And the city has no need of sun or

moon to shine upon it, for the glory of God is its light, and *its lamp is the Lamb*. By its light shall *the nations walk*; and the kings of the earth shall bring their glory into it..." (Rev. 21:22-24).

The Christian vision of hope today that invigorates and excites us consists of **his very presence in our lives** which eliminates any need for an external temple. We do not go to church or to the temple, *we have become the temple*. He lives in us. His glory has become part and parcel of our very personalities. This inner glory transforms us into day by day (II Cor. 3:15-18) makes up our light--the light we walk by. This serves as our center and core.

"And the kings of the earth shall bring their glory into it." The old model of eschatology has lots of problems with this. **Why** would you want the "glory" of the earthly kings to come into God's heaven? What among their "glory" would have value or use in that heaven? Yet if this describes the kingdom of God on earth today, if this describes the inter-nationalism of the kingdom, if this portrays how God's reign moves into the hearts and minds of men and women in all nations and *christianizes the best in their lives* so that they bring their glory into it--then it makes sense!

"They shall bring into it the glory and the honor of the nations. But nothing unclean shall enter it, nor any one who practices abomination or falsehood, but only those who are written in the Lamb's book of life." (Rev. 21:26-27).

When Christ's kingdom comes into the world, individually, person by person, by acceptance of him as King, it does not eliminate the kingdoms or governments of the world. It does something more important, more profound, and with more depth--*it kingdomizes those kingdoms*.

After all, the kingdom of God lies within as a spiritual phenomenon (Luke 17:20-21, Romans 14:17). When it comes, both the personal and collective kingdoms of this world give way. At individual and collective levels we begin *the transformational process* of acknowledging his lordship. With those facets of our lives that involve our honor and glory, we "bring it into" the holy city of Jerusalem.

Human civilization view historically from the first century to this century demonstrates this kingdomizing. Slowly, imperceptibly, the kingdom has infiltrated the enemy-occupied territory and slowly captured the minds and hearts (II Cor. 10:3-5) of those who give allegiance to Jesus. Western consciousness has become so Christianized that without this historical perspective many don't even recognize it. People speak about all the terrible and horrible things going on in the world today as if this indicates a worsening of things.

The problem with that perception apart from its negativity and rejection of the forces of goodness at work in the world? They only focus on a very minute part of human history. Most gloom-sayers only speak about a specific culture (USA) and contrast its time of political and religious conservatism (1950s) with its more liberal times that followed. If they would take a longer historical view and compare our cultural consciousness with that of the Greek-Roman consciousness of the first century, it would become evident immediately that "the knowledge of the Lord" has spread and covered the earth christianizing people (Hab. 2:14).

Even the most pagan people today who claim no religious affiliation would scream and protest bloody murder if we tossed newborn females out on the streets for the wolves, if we let our gladiators brutally mull and massacre each other as they did in the coliseums.

> "Then he showed me *the river of the water of life,* bright as crystal, flowing from the throne of God and of the Lamb, through the middle of the street of the city; also, on either side of the river, the tree of life with its twelve kinds of fruit, yielding its fruit each month; and the leaves of the tree for the healing of the nations." (Rev. 22:1-3).

Taking the preterist view gives me a vision of how the good-news of grace truly offers a sense of brotherhood, healing, forgiveness, equality, and cooperation to our world. This vision suggests the plenteous resources in the Judeo-Christian new covenant for healing the ugly hurtful breaches between the nations. After all, we all come from the same source, the same God, and our destiny involves each other. This messianic vision means beating our swords into plowshares and learning the ways of peace.

> "There shall no more be anything accursed, but the throne of God and of the Lamb shall be in it, and his servants shall worship him; they shall see his face, and his name shall be on their foreheads. And night shall be no more; they need no light of lamp or sun, for the Lord God will be their light, and they shall reign for ever and ever." (Rev. 22:4-5).

"Seeing his face," Hebraically, describes an intimate relationship. David forbid Absalom to "see his face" after Absalom killed his half-brother because David chose not to forgive and did not know how to fully come to terms with the evil in his own house (II Sam. 14:24-25). They had no fellowship. They shared nothing. But the Christian vision of hope for the new covenant messianic age speaks about becoming intimately related to God and experiencing his light. This reigning speaks of reigning abundantly in his grace (Romans 5:17).

When would all this happen? The angel said

> "'Do not seal up the words of the prophecy of this book, *for the time is near.*' ... 'Behold, *I am coming soon*, bringing my recompense to repay'... The Spirit and the Bride say, 'Come.' And let him who hears say, 'Come.' And let him who is thirsty come, let him who desires to take the water of life without price. ... *'Surely I am coming soon.'*" (Rev. 22:6-21).

John expected this first century vision of hope to occur soon. He expected it so soon, in fact, that he did not need to seal up of the vision. Previously, Daniel's vision existed a long way off into the future (namely, 500 years) when the messiah would come. The angel told him to seal up the words (Daniel 12). But not John. The time "was at hand" (Rev. 1:1).

QUESTIONS
ABOUT THE AD 70 REALIZED ESCHATOLOGY

Many questions may still remain. Making a major paradigm shift like this usually takes some time for all of the ramifications to shake down.

What Cure Do You Offer For Millennial Madness?

In an article in Christian research Journal (1990), Ron Rhodes says that

> "...over the past 2,000 years, the track record of those who have predicted and/or expected 'the end' has been **100% wrong**. The history of doomsday predictions is little more than a history of dashed expectations."

And, when people get caught up in frantic religious fervor of millennial madness and put all their hopes and expectations into some eschatological prediction basket, they can set themselves up for some major disappointment. They can seriously damage their very capacity for believing and hoping. "Hope deferred breaks the heart" (Proverbs 13:12).

Further, "those who succumb to millennial madness may end up making harmful decisions for their lives." Throughout history, such persons have sold all their possessions, headed for some mountain top with some guru, focused on building and equipping bomb shelters, interrupted their jobs, education, family, etc., left family and friends etc. *Millennial madness* tends to create an unsanity that prevents people from living in the here and now in God's great big beautiful world.

When the madness grows, it often tends to manifest itself in a paranoia. Everybody and everything different becomes a suspect. I have in my files newspaper and article clips about Kissinger, Saddam Hussain, J.F.K., and even Sears credit card(!), etc. as "the antichrist!" Such ridiculous conclusions discredit the speakers and their faith.

The millennial madness of "apocalypse now" has its appeal. After all, it does offer sensationalism! It feeds on prophetic speculations about the end, it develops *a reading into* any and all current affairs end-time signs. It provides a powerful fear motivation for speakers who need to keep people dependent on them for being "in the know" about the end times!

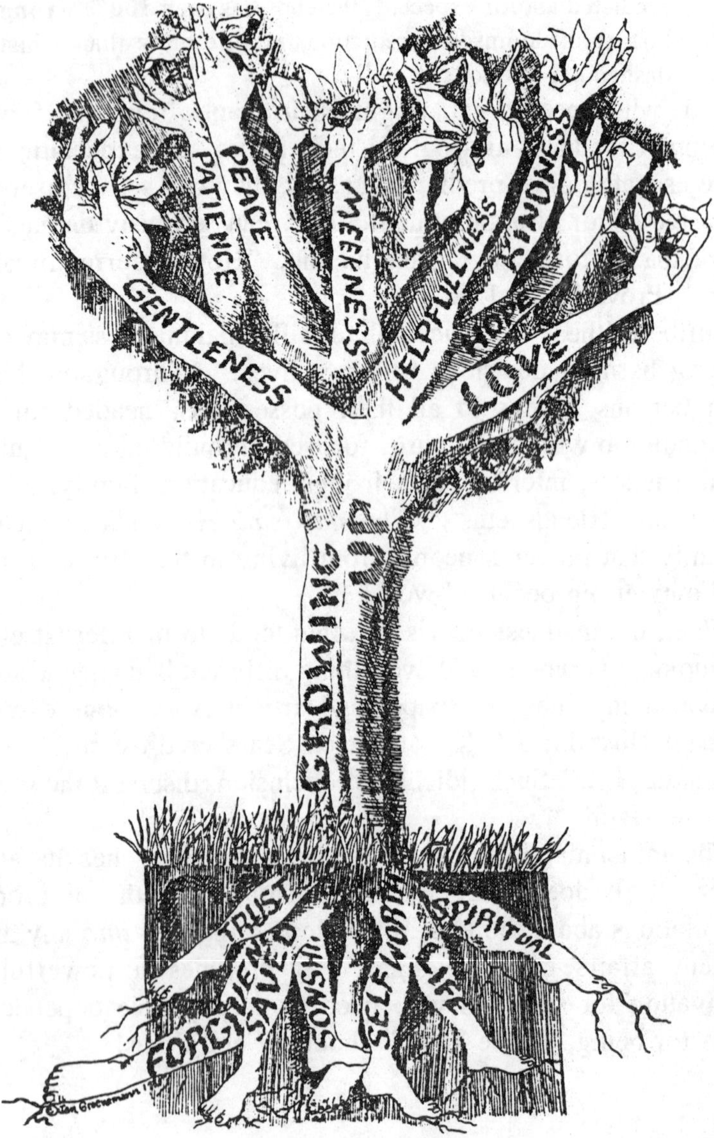
PEACE
PATIENCE
GENTLENESS
MEEKNESS
HELPFULLNESS
KINDNESS
HOPE
LOVE
GROWING
UP
TRUST
FORGIVENE
SAVED
SONSHI
SELF WORTH
SPIRITUAL
LIFE

Finale

INDEXING THE PSYCHOLOGICAL "MADNESS"

In Today's Churches About the So-called "End Times"

I entitled the original edition of this book "**The Cure for Millennial Madness**" because *when* we properly *index the biblical statements* about "the end of the world" that Jesus and his followers made, that indexing takes us to the first century, to the apostolic generation, and to the holocaust of Jerusalem and theocratic Israel in AD 70.

To do such cures us of all of the current sensational non-sense about us now living in "the end times" or about "the end of the world" coming soon. In this book I have dealt only with the biblical text rather than focusing on *the current "millennial madness"* of those who perceive our time as "the last days." To establish the context of those biblical statements undermines such current misapplications.

Now the issue of *"millennial madness,"* as a form of unsanity in so much of Christendom, describes an unhealthy attitude in my opinion. With the perception that "the end of the world" lies immediately at hand, that the "signs of the end" have begun to appear, and that the eschatology of the end-times will soon become fulfilled, numerous unpleasant and unsane consequences inevitably follow. These unsane consequences involve ways of thinking-feeling, behaving, and responding that comprise nothing else but psychological and spiritual *unsanity*.

I use the word *"unsanity"* intentionally to reference a specific meaning. "Insanity" serves as a legal term used to refer to those with such mental/emotional disorders that they cannot tell the real from what they imagine. They can't discern between information and concepts that arise inside their heads and those that come from without. As a result, they cannot make a good adjustment to reality. The courts declare a person "insane" who does not have enough discernment for sorting out reality.

Such lack of sanity refers to *a disordering within the mind-emotions* (and therefore speech and behaviors). When legitimate, the disorder arises from lacking the mechanisms of distinction that allows the rest of us to sort between what we internally see, hear, feel, smell and taste from what comes from the outside. If the "insane" *think* about killing mother, they can't tell if they did or didn't. They lack the internal mental mechanism for making (mapping) such distinctions.

By way of contrast, "sanity" refers to having the ability in *making a good adjustment to what exists* by developing and using the mental mechanisms for making crucial distinctions. The mental mapping of "reality" accords with the territory and enables one to make a good adjustment to it. The Bible describes such as a "right" or "sound" mind.

"Unsanity" refers to the entire continuum between lacking the ability to make distinctions that enables one to adjust to reality and the ability to make such. Alfred Korzybski (1933/1994) used this word in *"Science and Sanity"* to describe the problem that language plays in making good territory distinctions in our mental maps.

Biblically, I believe that *the Judeo-Christian perspective* of human nature, the world, God, ethics, etc. *makes for sanity and serenity*.

> "God has not given us the spirit of fear, but of power, love, and sound mind" (II Timothy 1:7).

Throughout scripture, those who "stay their mind on God" experience a perfect or complete peace (Isa. 26:3). Those who encounter Christ, though one may experience it as initially traumatic, develops the ability to recover one's "right mind" thereby enabling him to sit and learn from him (Mark 5:1-20).

This spirit of sanity and serenity gives one **a mental attitude of power** (courage, fortitude, resilience, mental strength, confidence, etc.), **love** (caring, extending oneself for the benefit of others, having a benevolent will, etc.) **and sound mind** (self-control, the ability to manage oneself) manifests itself more specifically in the fruit of the Spirit. True spirituality involves such expressions of mental-emotional health as love, joy, peace, longsuffering, gentleness, goodness, faith, meekness, and self-control (Gal. 5:23-24).

Millennial Unsanity

If we utilize these biblical descriptions as *criteria of good mental health,* then anything that generates a spirit of fearfulness, paranoia, negativism, gloom-and-doom, cynicism, impatience, etc. must not come from God. The attitude (or spirit) that God gives involves an attitude of proactivity wherein one assumes appropriate responsibility *for* self (accountability) and *to* others (relationship) and *to* the world (mission), that generates a positive and creative mind (reflecting the image of the Creator), and that models the life and behavior of Christ. He calls us to this.

How well then do some of the current books, churches, and programs that promote *"End Times" thinking-emoting* measure up to this biblical criteria? I don't think very well at all. I see as generating several *unsanities.*

The unsanity of negativism. In many Christian churches the emphasis on "the end times" generates an atmosphere of terror, dread, apprehensiveness, and paranoia. Some people become fanatical about the end coming, they intensely want and anticipate getting out of the world. Others become terrified about their versions of "the great tribulation" that they believe they must go through. They feel paranoid about anything and everything that they identify as "the mark of the beast," or the present "anti-Christ." Still others respond by depressing. They adopt a fatalistic attitude that they can do nothing, that the world "is getting worse and worse by the hour," and so they resign to the so-called "present darkness."

The negative attitude of such predominates to such an extent that many children of believers suffer from depression. They perceive that since the end will soon come, this cheats them out of having a life. Many end up resenting God for this. As a psychotherapist, I have seen numerous ones who stuffed their angers inside, who became increasingly passive (and passive-aggressive), who depressed, became phobic, panic-ridden, and even suicidal. They didn't handle the unsanity well.

The unsanity of paranoia. In some adults this unsanity manifests itself in *a general attitude of gloom-and-doom* which sees antichrist and the mark of the beast in every new development in the Near East. Every new development politically initiates a new round of books and seminars with "the truth" about the beast's true identity! Past books have targeted Hitler, Henry Kissinger, Nixon, every leader in Israel, in Egypt, in Russia, etc. People have identified the true "mark of the beast" as the Sears credit card, MasterCard, the ten-nation confederacy of the European Common Market, etc.

The unsanity of fanaticism. Some have become obsessed by various "end of the world" messages. These include the ones who join some of the eschatological cults and head out into communes, bunkers, and like the Essences of the first century, create a paramilitary organization that will survive the end. It includes those who current invest in money schemes in order to get a Temple rebuilt in Jerusalem so that Jesus can return and destroy it(!).

Others, like Hal Lindsey, not only create a panic and paranoia about the world coming to an end in our generation, falsely locating May 14, 1948 as the beginning of the end (*The Late Great Planet Earth*). But he also has set off a similar mania about the devil (*Satan is Alive and Well on Planet Earth*). Such millennial madness then becomes matched by **a devil mania** which teaches people to see demons and devils in every thing with which they disagree. If they don't like something, they label it as satanic, demonic, evil, etc.

What shall we say about all these unhappiness,

gloom-and-doom, bad-news people? I believe they have failed to index the biblical text and by so taking passages **out of context**, they have created this horrifying portrait of the future. But it only leaves them and their followers endowed with *a spirit of fear* rather than power, love, and sound mind. It leaves them fanatical, legalistic, and uninvolved in the ongoing political and social concerns of the world.

Dr. Desmond Ford, who has authored several works on *Revelation* and *Daniel,* describes this as *"Panic Theology."* This so frequently characterizes the way many people interpret *Revelation*. They first pull the entire book out of its first-century context and then declare without proof that the holocaust of the book will soon come upon this generation!

"There are no grounds for panic theology," Ford says in *Revelation* because John based it on "the pattern of the cross" in order to suggest consolation and assurance for the believer while judgment on those who reject the new covenant. That pinpoints the subject matter that *Revelation* reveals.

The unsanity of dreadful gloom. Even when "the Beast" and "the Dragon" did breathe down the neck of the early Christians during that interval period between the cross and AD 70, when the angels of judgment would soon pour out "the bowls of God's wrath" on the ungodly forces of the world--John wrote his *Revelation* to empower his recipients so that they could continue to live in a blessed or happy state (Rev. 1:3).

The *Apocalypse of Revelation* proclaims **a positive message about blessing and victory**, and in the context of worshipful celebration. John designed it to comfort and strengthen, to fortify and encourage, to brace up and excite his recipients. Those who use it to scare people *misuse* that holy word by not only taking it out of the time context (Rev. 1:1), but also out of the nature of the material context.

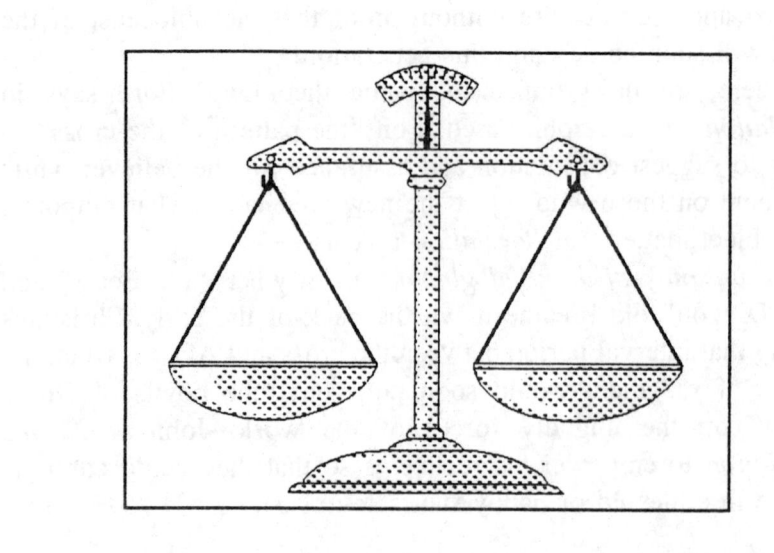

Appendix A

REALITY AND ITS SHADOWY PRECURSORS

*Exploring the Transition
From Old Covenant to New Covenant
Via the Biblical Metaphor of "Shadows--Reality"*

A *shadow* reflects the presence of a reality. To have a *shadow*, you have to have a *solid "substance"* that casts a shadow as it blocks light. When we identify something in the former age of law (Mosaic covenant) it suggests two things: the insubstantial nature of that item and simultaneously the substantial reality in the new covenant age. Old covenant "shadows" *foreshadowed* the coming reality of Christ as the following scriptures indicate.

"Therefore let no one pass judgment on you in questions of food and drink or with regard to a festival or a new moon or a sabbath. **These are only a shadow** of what is to come; but **the substance** belongs to Christ..." (Col. 2:16-17).

"For since the law has but **a shadow of the good things to come** instead of the true form of these realities..." (Heb. 10:1). "By this the Holy Spirit indicates that the way into the sanctuary is not yet opened as long as the outer tent is still standing (which is symbolic for the present age)..." (Heb. 9:8). "Priests...gifts... They serve **a copy and shadow** of the heavenly sanctuary..." (Heb. 8:4-5).

In the following list I have identified 29 old covenant *shadows* that imply 29 new covenant *realities*. These new covenant fulfillments indicate the spiritual "substance" that now inform and define Christian "reality."

Priests	→ Christians (I Peter 2:5,9)
High Priest	→ Christ (Heb. 10:21)
Temple, Physical, literal Temple of Solomon"	→ Christians (I Cor. 3:16-17)
	→ Temple is the Lamb" (Rev. 21:22)
Holy Place	→ Christians (I Cor. 6:19-20)
Most Holy Place	→ Presence of God (Heb. 10:19-23)
Shekinah of Glory	→ Presence of God/Holy Spirit/Jesus

(John 1:14-18)

Sacrifice/s	→ Committed life of believers (Rom. 12:1-2)
Alter	→ Christ (Heb. 13:10)
Lamb/Pascal Lamb	→ Christ (I Cor. 5:7)
Incense offered	→ Prayers of believers (Rev. 5:8)
Laver of washing	→ The washing of regeneration (Titus 3:5)
Sprinkling of Blood	→ Cleansing/Covenanting (Heb. 9:13-14)
PassoverJudgment Day/	→ Time of the Cross (John 12:31-32)
Passover Feast/Meal Actual wine/bread	→ Wine/Bread of Christ-- body & blood (John 6)
Rituals: priests "performing ritual of duties"	→ Christ finishing the work redemption (Heb. 9:6)(Heb. 10:1-15)
Mercy-seat shadowed by angels	→ Christ, esp. his tomb (John 20)
Torah written on Tables of Stone	→ God's Covenant written on our hearts (II Cor. 3:3-6, Heb. 8:6-13)
Veil	→ Flesh of Christ split (Heb. 10:19-21)
Lampstand in Temple	→ Christ is the light (Rev. 23:23-24)
Feast of Tabernacles	→ Christ's life giving water/Holy Spirit (John 7:1-2, 37-39)
Sabbath	→ Rest/peace of Christ (Matt. 11:28-30)
Sabbaths, New Moons, holy days	→ All days holy (Rom. 14:1-12, Col. 2:16f)
Canaan Rest/Sabbath Rest	→ Peace of Christ (Heb. 4:1-16)
King / Kingdom	→ Christ/ Christians (I Pet. 2:5.9, Rev. 5:8-9)
Prophet	→ Christ (Heb. 1:1-3)
Old Covenant	→ New covenant (Jer. 31:31-34, Heb. 8:5-13)
Ritual forgiveness	→ Actual, completed forgiveness (Rom. 5:1, 8:1-4) "No condemnation"
Resurrection of body	→ Spiritual resurrection from sin-death (Rom. 6, I Cor. 15)

What Significance Does this Suggest?

If the reality of the new covenant age and its promises has come--then today in this new covenant age we have (and need) no physical, literal, actual...

> • *Temple or building*--since we comprise God's temple and God dwells in us.
> • Priests or holy men conducting services--since we comprise a

nation of priests and have access to God via Jesus Christ as our mediator (I Timothy 2:4-5).

- *Services of a ritualistic nature*--since Jesus has become our way into the presence of God. His "service" satisfied heaven "once and for all" (Hebrews 10:1-23).
- *Physical, literal festivities* (i.e. new moons, sabbaths, holy days)--since Jesus comprises our Rest, our New Year, Our Light, Life, Celebration, Booth, etc. Now the festivity lies in him!
- *Sacramental rituals* ("visible means of invisible grace")--since in him we have received "grace upon grace" (John 1:16). His life ("blood" and "body") comprise *the sacraments* (means of grace) and sustains us completely. This eliminates the need for "sacraments" in the sense of such externals functioning as the **means** for receiving grace.
- *Physical, literal "Book" or "Stone Tables" of God*--since He has written his new covenant on our hearts by his spirit. The so-called "New Testament" only serves as a book **about** the new covenant, not the covenant itself (II Cor. 3:3-6, John 5:39).
- *Physical, literal resurrection of body*--since we have already become resurrected--spiritually--in him and the new "body" of believers from old and new covenants have experienced resurrection into his new life.
- *Physical, literal second coming*--since he has already come to judge "heaven and earth" and bring an end to the old covenant world.

We now conclude that the kingdom completely exists within us (Luke 17:20-21), compromised of elements not of meat and drink (Rom. 14:17), not written on tables of stone, but fleshly tables of the heart, a ministration of life and spirit and transformation (II Cor. 3:3-18).

This shifts everything. *It puts ultimate emphasis on "spirituality"* (Gal. 6:1, 5:22-23)--on the "heart" --on the inward person, not on the outward person. It makes our "spiritual worship" not a matter of so-called "church going" but of commitment living (Rom. 12:1-2ff). This makes *assembling* with other believers **not** a matter of "going to church" because we "are" (exists as) "church" before and after we "go." Assembling in the Christian age no longer serves as our "spiritual worship," but as a place for social encouragement, learning, edification, etc.

Other Available Resources

E.T. Publications has several publications dealing with theology, hermeneutics, eschatology, etc.

- *"Revelation: An Oracle of the End."*
- *Hermeneutics: Literary Devices that Open Up the Biblical Text."*
. *"Transitional Christianity's Evolution"* **by Doug Adams.**
- Dynamic View of Scripture.
- *Christian Resourcefulness* (Epistle of Philippians).
- *More Fundamental than Obedience.*
- *Understanding "Hell" Via the Gospel.*
- *The "Demon" Phenomenon* (So-called "Possession").
- *Case Study of Judas* (The Evil of Manipulation).
- *Case Study of Saul* (When Personality Goes to Hell).
- *Mastering Spiritual Trauma* (1993 #5).
- *Biblical Case Studies of Trauma Recovery* (1993 #4).
- *NLP & the Judeo-Christian Perspective* (1991, #1).
- *NLP & the New Age Movement* from the Judeo-Christian Perspective (with Dr. Carl Lloyd).
- *Emotions: Sometimes I Have Them/Sometimes They Have Me!* (1985). Begins with a case study of King David and the emotional mess that he made when he didn't effectively manage his emotions. $8.00
- *Motivation: How to Become a Positive Force in a Negative World.* (1987). A study of how to not "lose heart" but maintain a "heartful," courageous, and highly motivated response to life. $8.00
- *Speak Up, Speak Clear, Speak Kind.* (1987). 100 pages on communication principles, skills, strategies, and dynamics. $5.00
- *How to Get Yourself Really Motivated.* (1988). Follow-up to the book on motivation that identifies 38 motivational skills incorporating the NLP strategy approach. $5.00
- *Meta-States: A Domain of Logical Levels, Self-Reflexiveness in Human States of Consciousness.* (1995). An award-winning developing in the field of NLP about consciousness when it generates states-about-states and opens up "transcendence" as a legitimate part of human psychology. $20.00
- *Dragon Slaying: From Dragons to Princes.* (1996). A more readable and popular version of "Meta-States" created from transcripts of the

workshop by the same name. Focuses on enabling a person to slay and/or tame their "dragon" states and to develop state management skills. $20.00.

OTHER SOURCES OF PRETERIST WRITINGS

I wrote this to present a brief overview of the preterist viewpoint about Christian eschatology. By design I wanted to offer this empowering perspective in a succinct format to show the value and power of the preterist view. If this has aroused your interest and you want to read more, then let me refer you to some other materials.

- **Eschatology Publications:** The Journal *"The Living Presence"* 4705 Parkman Rd NW, Warren, OH 44481 ($10 yearly). "The Spirit of Prophecy," Max R. King ($6.95). "The Cross and the Parousia of Christ," Max R. King ($18.95). "II Peter 3: The Late Great Kingdom," Don K. Preston ($6.50).
- **Kingdom Publications** publishes a quarterly preterist journal, *"Kingdom Counsel"* edited by Edward E. Stevens ($18 yearly). They also make available *The Parousia* by J. Stuart Russell ($17.00 postpaid), "Josephus: Complete Works" ($18.00 postpaid), "What Happened in AD 70?" by Ed Stevens ($6.00 postpaid), and over forty other fine preterist publications. They have a web site on the internet which can be found by searching for "preterist." Call or write for a book and tape list: (122 Seaward Ave, Bradford, PA 16701, Phone: 814-368-6578).
- **Joy of the Lord,** pamphlets and materials from the preterist view: *Rev. Arthur Melanson,* especially his brochure, "Questions and Answers About Realized Eschatology." (PO Box 237, Audubon, NJ 08106.)
- **John L. Bray Ministry, Inc.**, well-researched 294-page book, Matthew 24 Fulfilled. $15 including postage. John Bray has many other fine preterist booklets available. (PO Box 90129, Lakeland, FL 33804.
- **International Preterist Association**: Monthly Newsletter about the Preterist Movement throughout the world. PO Box 7, Castle Rock, CO. 80104-0007. (303) 660-1752. Founded by Rev. Tom Joseph and Dr. L. Michael Hall.

BIBLIOGRAPHY

Aytoun, Robert A. *City Centres of Early Christianity.* London: Hodder and Stroughton, 1915.

Beasley-Murray, G. R. *The Book of Revelation,* New Century Bible Commentary. Grand Rapids, MI: Eerdmans, 1974.

Bonhoeffer, Dietrich. *The Cost Of Discipleship.* (Trans. Charles Kaiser Verlag Munchen). New York: Macmillan Co., 1937/1970.

Brandon, S .G. F. *The Fall Of Jerusalem And The Christian Church: A Study Of The Effects Of The Jewish Overthrow Of AD 70 On Christianity.* London, 1951.

Brandon, S .G. F. *Jesus And The Zealots: A Study Of The Political Factor In Primitive Christianity.* Manchester Univ. Press, 1967.

Brinsmead, Robert D. "The Apocalyptic Spirit," *Verdict 4: #2* (Feb. 1981). Fallbrook, California: Verdict: A Journal of Theology, 1981.

Charles, R. H. *A Critical And Exegetical Commentary On Revelation.* New York: Charles Scribners, 1920.

Collins, Adela Yarbro. *The Combat Myth In The Book Of Revelation.* Massachusetts: Scholars Press, 1976.

Collins, Adela Yarbro. *Crisis and Catharsis: The Power of the Apocalypse,* 1984.

Collins, Adela Yarbro. *The Apocalypse.* Wilmington, Delaware: Michael Glazier, Inc., 1986.

Corsini, Eugenio. *The Apocalypse: The Perennial Revelation Of Jesus Christ.* (Trans. by Francis J. Moloney). Wilmington, DE: Michael Glazier, Inc., 1983.

Elliott-Binns, L. E. *Galilean Christianity: Studies in Biblical Theology.* Alec R. Allenson Inc., 1956.

Ellul, Jacques. *Apocalypse.* (Trans. by George W. Schreiner). New York: Seabury Press, 1977.

Faulkner, John A. *Crises In The Early Church*. New York: 1912.

Furneaux, Rupert. *The Roman Siege of Jerusalem*. New York: David McKay Co., 1972.

Farrar, Frederic W. *Early Days of Christianity*. New York: Cassell Petter, Galpin & Co., 1882.

Farrer, Austin. *A Rebirth Of Images*. Boston, Massachusetts: Beacon Press, 1963.

Ford, J. Massyingberde. *Revelation: Anchor Bible*. New York: Doubleday, 1975.

Ford, Desmond. *Crisis! A Commentary On The Book Of Revelation*. Newcastle, California: Desmond Ford Publications, 1982.

Gaston, Lloyd. *No Stone On Another: Studies In The Significance Of The Fall Of Jerusalem In The Synoptic Gospels*. Leiden, Netherlands: E. J. Brill, 1970.

Hanson, Paul D. "Visionaries And Their Apocalypses." *Issues in Religion and Theology, 41*. Philadelphia, Pennsylvania: Fortress Press, 1983.

Hereford, Robert T. *The Pharisees*. Boston, MA: Beacon Press, 1962.

Jenkins, Ferrell. *The Old Testament In The Book Of Revelation*. Indiana: Cogdill Found. Pubs., 1972.

Jeske, Richard L. (1983). *Revelation For Today: Images Of Hope*. Philadelphia, PA: Fortress Press, 1983.

Kasemann, Ernest. *Commentary on Romans*. (Trans. & ed. by Geoffrey Bromiley). Grand Rapids, Michigan: Eerdmans, 1980.

King, Max R. *The Spirit Of Prophecy*. Warren, Ohio: Research & Writing Ministry, 1971/1990.

King, Max. *The Cross And The Parousia Of Christ: The two dimensions of one age-changing eschaton*. Warren, Ohio: Research & Writing Ministry, 1987.

Kock, Klaus. *The Rediscovery Of Apocalyptic: Studies In Biblical Theology #22*. Illinois: Alen Allenson, 1970.

Ladd, George Eldon. *A Commentary On The Revelation.* Grand Rapids, MI: Eerdmans Publications, 1972.

Matthews, Shailer. *A History Of New Testament Times In Palestine: 175 BC -- 70 AD.* MacMillan, 1918.

Minear, Paul. *I Saw A New Earth: An Introduction To The Visions Of The Apocalypse.* Washington: Corpus Books, 1968.

Minear, Paul. *New Testament Apocalyptic.* Abingdon, 1981.

Ogden, Arthur M. *The Avenging Of The Apostles And Prophets.* Louisville, Kentucky, 1985.

Pilch, John J. *What Are They Saying About The Book Of Revelation.* New York: Paulist Press, 1978.

Preston, Don K. *II Peter 3: The Late Great Kingdom.* Ardmore, OK: Don Preston Publications, 1990.

Robinson, John A. T. *Redating The New Testament.* Philadelphia, PA: Westminster Press, 1976.

Russell, James Stuart. *The Parousia: A Critical Inquiry Into The New Testament Doctrine Of Our Lord's Second Coming.* Bradford, PA: Kingdom Publications, 1996.

Russell, D. S. *The Method And Message Of Jewish Apocalyptic.* Philadelphia, PA: Westminster Press, 1964.

Schmithals, Walter. *The Apocalyptic Movement: Introduction And Interpretation.* Abingdon Press, 1973.

Stevens, Edward E. *What Happened In AD 70?* Bradford, PA: Kingdom Publications, 1997.

Sweet, J.P.M. *Revelation: Westminster Pelican Commentary.* Philadelphia, PA: Westminster Press, 1979.

Thackeray, H. St. J. (Trans.). *The Book Of The Wars Of The Jews By Josephus.* Massachusetts: Harvard University Press.

Torrey, Charles C. *The Apocalypse Of John*. Boston: Yale University Press, 1958.

Wallace, Foy E., Jr. *The Book Of Revelation: A Commentary On The Apocalypse Of The New Testament*. Fort Worth, TX: Foy E. Wallace, Jr. Publications, 1966.

Workman, Herbert B. *Persecution In The Early Church: A Chapter In The History Of Renunciation*. London: Epworth Press, 1906.

About this book---

APOCALYPSE THEN VS. APOCALYPSE IN THE NEAR FUTURE

To list to some people talk, we would think that only *one* perspective exists in the Christian community about the apocalypse of "the end of the world." "Christian" Television and radio often also portrays this impression.

Yet actually, from Amillennialists, Postmillennialists, Premillennialists, to Pan-millennialists (it will all pan out in the end!), *many different viewpoints exist* about eschatology and about the Apocalypse.

In this book you will find what most people would consider a *new* eschatological perspective--one that nicely integrates covenant theology with "the good-news of the grace of God" into the historical context out of which our NT scriptures arose.

Based upon the text of the Bible, this view applies the hermeneutic principle of **indexing** the words, language, and referents of the Bible to the author, recipients, and day in which it arose. Letting the good-news of the new covenant determine the big picture--**Apocalypse Then** avoids getting lost in the details.

This view also presents a psychologically sound interpretation--an interpretations that fits with the criteria that *"God has **not** given us the spirit of fear, but of power, and love, and sound mind"* (II Tim. 1:7). Any eschatological viewpoint that creates morbid fearfulness, dread, apprehension, and unresourcefulness cannot represent a healthy Christian view. Any viewpoint that leaves people scared of *Revelation*, timid about living life fully in God's great big wonderful world, and unsure about their salvation (forgiveness, renewal, transformation, etc.), does not comprise the "shalom" (wholeness/ peace) that the true gospel brings.

Whether you agree or disagree with the position held here--it should get you to *think*, to re-examine the biblical text itself, and deepen your appreciation of the grace of Covenant, the glory of the gospel, and your appreciation of first century history.

About the Author--

Dr. L. Michael Hall received ordination in a conservative "undenominational" denomination and spent ten years in various pastorate ministries (1970s). During that time he became interested in pastoral psychology--in applying the rich biblical truths of the Judeo-Christian faith to everyday "psychological" (mental-emotional) concerns. Simultaneously, his Greek and Hebrew linguistic studies captivated his interest in the role that language itself plays in human consciousness. Eventually, he earned a Ph.D. in cognitive-behavioral psychology with an emphasis in linguistics. His dissertation concerned the linguistics that bring healing in the context of psychotherapy using the formulations of general-semantics. He has authored numerous works in theology, psychology, and linguistics.

Other books by Michael Hall:

Emotions: Sometimes I Have Them/Sometimes They Have Me! (1985)
Motivation: How to Be a Positive Force in a Negative World (1987)
Speak Up, Speak Clear, Speak Kind (1987)
How to Really Get Yourself Motivated Skill-Book (1988)
The Cure For Millennial Madness (1994)
Meta-States: Self-Reflexiveness in Human States of Consciousness (1995)
Dragon Slaying: Dragons to Princes (1986)
The Spirit of NLP: The Process, Meaning & Criteria For Mastering NLP (1996)
Languaging: The Linguistics of Psychotherapy, How Language Works... (1996)
Patterns For Renewing the Mind with NLP (With Dr. Bodenhamer) (1997)
Time-Lining: Advanced Patterns Processes (With Dr. Bodenhamer) (1997)
Neuro-Linguistic Programming: The Next Step into Logical Levels (1977)

Coming Soon--

Over My Dead Body!
The 4th. Gospel From a Preterist Viewpoint

Suppose for a moment that someone wrote the fourth gospel (commonly called "John") to the Jewish Leaders of the first century-- prior to the Fall of Jerusalem with the message of Good-news *to warn them about the coming End of their World!*

Suppose further that that somebody commanded some respect within that community of the educated Sanhedrin leaders. Suppose that "beloved disciple" "was known to the high priest" (18:15) so much that he could easily enter into the high priest's quarters and even get Peter admitted!

Suppose that he too had long resisted Jesus and the Jesus movement even though his very sisters had jumped on board for many of the same reasons that Nicodemus, Joseph, and other Sanhedrin members held back.

Yet suppose this young Jewish Leader had a heart of spirituality that touched Jesus so much that Jesus "loved him" (11:3-4). Suppose that he died and then experienced first-hand *the resurrection power of Jesus of Nazareth!*

Then suppose that he decided to write **"The Jerusalem Gospel"** (our Fourth Gospel) with all the quality of the highest and most developed Greek--using Rabbinical linguistic devices in order to present **Seven Signs** pointing to Jesus as the Messiah. Suppose this beloved disciple, who did not "go into all the world" as did the Apostles, but who stayed in Jerusalem with Jesus' mother Mary as his permanent guest (19:25-27) then decided to write a gospel to explain the reasons for the initial conflict between the Jewish leadership and the Jewish Messiah.

Then we might have a document from someone who knew firsthand what it felt like to stubbornly think, **"It'd be over my dead body** before I give my allegiance to that Galilean prophet...!"

This provocative work posits that Lazarus wrote the Fourth Gospel, prior to AD 70, as a final warning about the judgment of the world of theocratic Israel.

Coming Soon